YOU CAN LEAD AN ATHEIST TO EVIDENCE BUT YOU CAN'T MAKE HIM THINK

You Can Lead an Atheist to Evidence But You Can't Make Him Think

ANSWERS TO QUESTIONS FROM ANGRY SKEPTICS

By Ray Comfort

WND Books

YOU CAN LEAD AN ATHEIST TO EVIDENCE, BUT YOU CAN'T MAKE HIM THINK
A WND Books book
Published by WorldNetDaily
Los Angeles, CA
Copyright © 2009 by Ray Comfort

Jacket design by Lynn Copeland

WND Books are distributed to the trade by:
Midpoint Trade Books
27 West 20th Street, Suite 1102
New York, NY 10011

WND Books are available at special discounts for bulk purchases. WND Books, Inc. also publishes books in electronic formats. For more information call (310) 961-4170 or visit www.wndbooks.com.

First Edition

ISBN 13-Digit: 9781935071068
ISBN 10-Digit: 1935071068
E-Book ISBN 13-Digit: 9781935071594
E-Book ISBN 10-Digit: 1935071599
Library of Congress Control Number: 2008940362

Printed in the United States of America

10 9 8 7 6 5 4 3 2

To all those who see and think.

TABLE OF CONTENTS

Dear Reader,

A few months before learning of Ray's intention to publish this book, I watched a debate over the resurrection of Christ between Dr. Anthony Flew and Dr. Gary Habermas. What surprised me most about this debate wasn't the exquisite arguments presented from these powerful philosophical minds, but a comment from Dr. Habermas about Dr. Flew—then an atheist, and at the time of this writing still a non-Christian Deist—being a dear friend and even tucking in his children at night.

The close friendship between these two people with polar opposite worldviews is now almost entirely a relic of the past. Gone are the days when people like Larry Flynt and Jerry Falwell can make amends and be friends; in are the days when hacks can make films charging a two-thousand-year-old religion with being part of a global conspiracy that controls world banks and "covers up" tragedies like 9/11.

Although nobody is justified with befriending those whose worldviews are outright dangerous, such as a Hitler or a bin Laden, respecting those who hold opposing beliefs often opens up ways to examine the consistency of what you hold and to consider the truth claims of what others hold in as neutral of an atmosphere as possible.

With the advent of "New Atheism," hostility and ridicule have all but replaced open, honest discussion. Scholarly and philosophical analysis have taken a back seat to pop polemics, and the biggest names in the movement have subsequently banished the art of philosophical study to make sure their diatribes sell. Christians are simply called idiots, fools, and fanatics, yet the actual arguments that the most well-known New Atheist books present demonstrate the same lack of both logic and knowledge that they carelessly paste on Christianity. The best (and subsequently the most respectful) critical books are relegated to distant shelves deep in the shadow of these "challenging" rants, which are propped at the front door of any bookstore for all to see and buy.

After all, it's name calling, and not thinking, that brings home the bucks.

It is now time for Christianity to bite back at the so-called Brights. Although I may not agree with everything Ray says in this book, I do agree that the recent popularization of atheism is unkind, uncritical, and uninformed. Although most in this movement will only scoff at the cover of this book and leave it unread on the shelves, some may decide to pick it up just to laugh at its contents. My advice to such people is to leave this attitude behind—instead, I challenge you to turn these pages with a clear and critical mind. Even if Ray himself uses polemics in this book, look past it, look at his logic, and answer it by leaving your emotion behind.

Nobody can "make" anyone else think; they choose that for themselves, but if you choose instead to laugh or yell, you're proving the spirit of the title of this book correct. You likely think you can prove Ray wrong—here's your chance. Are you up for the challenge?

Darrin Rasberry, Atheist

Most who profess atheism aren't really "atheists." After a few moments chatting with them about the fact that every building is proof that there was a builder, and that creation therefore is proof that there is a Creator, many change their minds.

But then there's the *staunch* atheist. This one is a challenge. He is the marlin of deep-sea fishing, and he doesn't give up easily. As a fisher of men, I have found that this type of atheist is always ready for debate. He will take the bait, the hook, and any line you give him, and give you a run for your money.

The staunch atheist has the zeal of a religious fanatic. He is fundamentalist in his belief that there is no God—and, armed with basic Richard Dawkins phrases, he is ready for a fight. He is unreasonable, angry, and bitter at God, and will color his speech with blasphemy of His name, despite the fact that he professes that God doesn't exist. The atheist is someone who pretends that there is no God.

Late in 2007, a courageous Christian dropped a handful of booklets I published called *The Atheist Test* at a gathering of staunch atheists.[1] These people were so committed to the belief that God didn't exist they met once a month at the local IHOP (International House of Prayer?) at the John Wayne Airport in Orange County, California.

When they found out that I authored the booklet, they kindly invited me to join them for dinner on January 8, 2008. They requested that I get there an hour early to "set a baseline," because some of their members "do get a bit hot-headed when discussing religion." I accepted their invitation and decided to take my manager with me. Mark Spence is the dean of the "School of Biblical Evangelism."[2]

Before we went, I received permission from them to also take a handheld HD camera.[3] I was determined not to go there to win an argument, but to simply show that I deeply cared for them as people, as most atheists in this category have the impression that Christians don't like them.

We arrived about five minutes early, shook hands, and sat down. After the orders were taken, I quietly approached the waiter and told him to give me the bill for the entire party. When he brought it to me I was almost shaking with excitement. If someone had tried to take it from me I would have physically fought them. I felt like I used to feel with my kids early on Christmas morning. When the group found out that I had personally paid the tab they were very grateful, polite, pleasant, kind, and extremely thankful (see 1 Peter 2:15). The experience was a highlight of my life.

Then about ten of us huddled around a table and talked about the things of God for about an hour. It was up close and personal. Mark Spence answered every question and objection they had, calmly and eloquently.

I took copies of my new book, *How to Know God Exists*, and all the folks at our table wanted one (it's a strange feeling signing books for atheists). Then we posed for pictures and left, almost bursting with joy after such a wonderful opportunity to meet and talk with these dear people.

Some atheists are nasty. Some are nice. One thing I do know: *all* atheists are lost, and they desperately need a Savior. That's why I wrote this book. I hope you find it helpful.

The following questions were taken directly from my blog.[4] Each atheist who comments has been told: "Cuss words (mild or abbrev.), blasphemy, URLs, incivility, or failure to give the names 'God' or 'Jesus' capitals will be deleted."

Ray Comfort
Los Angeles, California

I am grateful to WorldNetDaily (particularly to my friend Joseph Farah) for seeing the importance of addressing this vital issue at this time in human history.

To be an atheist is to play Russian roulette with all barrels loaded. An atheist can't win. Of course, he feels and acts like a big player, until the trigger is pulled.

The issue isn't the existence of God. If the atheist is wrong and there is a Creator, then he was wrong. He gambled and he lost. No big deal. The real gamble is that there's no hell. That's what makes the player sweat just a little. "What if?" is the deep and nagging doubt. He believes it's worth the excitement of the game. Yet atheism isn't a mind game; it is intellectual suicide.

We know that there are six bullets that aim right into the brain of humanity:

1. *Creation*. Could you believe that the book you are holding came into being without an author? There was nothing. No paper, no ink. No cardboard. No editor. No author. There was nothing, and then a Big Bang changed everything. Time (the magic ingredient) produced a book with a cover, binding, coherent words, page numbers, and chapters, all in perfect order. Such thoughts are truly insane. You cannot have order without intelligence creating order. And there cannot be an ordered creation without an intelligent Creator.

2. *The God-given conscience*. All sane people have a conscience. It comes with the package. It is an inbuilt judge in the courtroom of the mind. It makes moral judgments, even when its voice is not wanted, and its voice *only* addresses that which is moral. It doesn't speak when my tie doesn't match my shirt. But it does speak when I steal a tie from a store. Why is that? Where did the conscience come from? Why do all civilizations have the knowledge that it's wrong to lie, kill, steal, etc.? Our social surroundings may shape the conscience, but they

don't create it. It is the inner light that God has given to every one of us, and it leaves us without excuse for our sin.

3. *The unchanging testimony of Holy Scripture.* Do what they will to the testimony of Scripture—paint it as an ancient and archaic book, say it is full of mistakes, that it has been changed down through the ages, that it says that the earth is flat—but it remains the unchanging Word of the Living God. It is His Book, and it is a lamp to our feet and a light to our path. Refuse its wisdom, and you walk in darkness at your own peril.

4. *The true and faithful testimony of the genuine Christian.* These are not people who believe in God. Rather, they are sinners who have come to know Him. The Christian is called to testify as a witness to the truth. As in a court of law, the judge doesn't want poetic or flowery speech. He simply wants to hear what the witness has seen and heard. It is then up to the jury to believe or not believe his testimony. The atheist chooses not to believe the testimony of the Christian, and in doing so, accuses him of bearing false witness. But why would a Christian lie? Why would he want to be found a liar, when the Book in which he sincerely believes warns that all liars will be cast into the lake of fire?

5. *The witness of Jesus Christ.* The True and Faithful Witness, before Whom every knee shall bow. The challenge to any atheist is to read the testimony of Scripture. Any honest skeptic will have no choice but to come to the conclusion that "never a man spoke like this Man." He claimed to be God in human form. He claimed to have the power to raise all of humanity at the resurrection of the dead, with His lone voice. He claimed to be pre-existent, and that He came down to this earth to do the will of God. To make such claims, He could only have been a simpleton (that doesn't match His matchless words), a liar (that doesn't match His impeccable moral teaching), insane (then billions down through the ages have followed the teachings of a madman), or He was who He said He was.

6. *The Spirit of Almighty God* watches every thought and every deed and will bring every work into judgment, including every secret thing, whether it is good or evil. No one will get away with a thing. No murderer will go unpunished. No rapist will get away with rape. Perfect justice will be done. But the justice of Almighty God is so

thorough He will see to it that thieves, liars, fornicators, blasphemers, adulterers, and all who have transgressed the moral Law (the Ten Commandments) will get equity—that which is due to them.

Death is the trigger that will send eternal justice like a speeding bullet into the heart of the sinner. It will end the game of life in a heartbeat, and no second chance will come. So, if you are an atheist, let me reason with you. You cannot win. Think about your life. Think about eternity, while you still have time.

Chapter One

CREATION MUST
HAVE A CREATOR

"It would be very difficult to explain why the universe should have begun in just this way, except as the act of a God who intended to create beings like us."[1]

—STEPHEN HAWKING

theists' beliefs vary as much as atheists themselves. Still, atheists hold a fundamental belief that unifies them. An "atheist" *believes* that there is no God and that man came into being without any intelligent design. If there was no designer, then an atheist owes his existence to random chance, over millions or billions of years, of course. While some believers in evolution deny that evolution is a random process, if it's not unplanned, then it's planned. And if it is planned, then there is Someone doing the planning.

Let's be a fly on the wall as man evolves as an unplanned being. We will give him a generic name, just to make it easier for us to refer to him. Let's call him "Adam." As a fly on the wall, we are there when Adam takes his first breath. It is fortunate that, when his lungs drew in the air that surrounded him, the air was there. If there had been no air, he wouldn't have been able to breathe and he would have instantly died. But for some reason it was there, presumably at 14.7 pounds per square inch.

But it's more miraculous than the air just being there. It was fortunate the air was made up of 78.09 percent nitrogen and 20.95 percent oxygen—the exact mixture that his lungs and blood needed to survive. Without that oxygen Adam would have gasped, and his first breath would have been his last. What a miracle of chance that oxygen existed in just the right percentage to maintain Adam's life, and the life of his wife, whom we will give the generic name "Eve." She needed to be around to procreate the Adamic race. It's another amazing miracle that she evolved (with lungs) by chance over millions of years to maturity, at the same time as Adam.

It was also an amazing coincidence that gravity existed at the time of their evolution. Without it, the first man and his first mate would have spun off into the infinitude of space. But for some reason it evolved and matured at just the right time to keep their feet firmly planted on the earth, which also evolved.

Another fantastic happenstance: the fact that Adam and his companion not only evolved a thirst for liquid that they had never tasted, but the needed life-giving water also evolved for them at just the right time. Without its quenching ability, they would have dried out and died out.

Another incredible twist of Providence was that light existed. Somehow the sun evolved and set itself at 93 million miles away from Planet Earth. Without light, Adam and Eve wouldn't have been able to see each other, to come together for procreation, so that they could bring forth offspring after their own kind. But the light wasn't just for them to see each other. Without it, they would have starved to death, because the food that had evolved could not have existed without photosynthesis. A process which itself evolved over the years.

Bear in mind that an atheist believes that all these miraculous coincidences took place by chance. But he doesn't just believe that man and woman came into being without a Creator, but that *all of creation* did—amazing flowers, massive trees, succulent fruits, beautiful birds, the animal kingdom, the sea, fish, natural laws, etc. His faith is much greater than mine. I could never for a moment believe that all these things happened by chance. Never in a million years. But the believing atheist does, and he amazingly looks down intellectually on those that maintain that all this incredible creation wasn't an accident at all, but the act of an incredible Creator.[2]

Hi Ray, I grew up Christian, but have recently been struggling with the existence of an omnipresent, unconditional God…. I understand. He wants us to choose to love Him. For me, it's not a question of evolution or creation. I just have an abject fear that God doesn't exist. In your opinion, does this make me a "false convert"? Do you struggle with doubt? Do you have any suggestions for someone like me?

You need not fear. Just say this to yourself: "Every building has a builder." You can't have a building without a builder (try to think of one). Buildings don't happen by themselves. It's impossible. "For every house is built by some man…" (Hebrews 3:4). The same principle applies to paintings and painters. The painting is absolute proof that there is a painter (try to think of a painting that didn't have a painter). Paintings don't happen by themselves. It's impossible. Here's my point. Creation is *absolute* proof that there is a Creator. You cannot have a creation without a Creator. It is impossible ("Then who made God?" has a logical answer). End of argument; unless, according to the Bible, you are a fool (read Psalm 14:1 and Romans 1:20).

To address your other question—do I struggle with doubt? Never. I would *never* for a moment doubt the existence of God because of the evidence of creation. I would never doubt the reality of God because, in a moment of time, He transformed my life. And I would never doubt the character of God because I trust His integrity implicitly. The Bible says that if you doubt God, you call Him a liar (see 1 John 5:10). If I doubt you when you tell me something, it's an insult to your integrity. It means I think that you are a liar. So never doubt God. Trust Him with all your heart, even when trust seems impossible. Those are the times when faith comes in (see Proverbs 3:5).

You err when you compare a "building and its builder" with a "human and his creator;" they are not the same thing!

Actually, it's not me who says that every building has a builder and that logically leads to the truth that creation therefore proves that there is a Creator. God's Word makes the intellectual condescension to make the obvious comparison. It says, "For every house is built by some man; but he that built all things is God" (Hebrews 3:4).

When someone becomes a Christian, he immediately cares about those around him. He cares about those unwanted in society—the poor, the bad, and the ugly (those who lack what society esteems). This is because God put His love within him the moment that he repented and trusted the Savior.

It is because of God's love that I care about the fate of atheists. When an atheist says he sees no evidence that God exists, I take the time to reason with him about creation not being an accident, even though it is intellectually demeaning to have to do so (atheism is the epitome of stupidity). It's an intellectual embarrassment. But I have done so thousands of times, and will do so until my last breath…thanks alone to the love of God that dwells in me.

It's incredible that the mind can do so many things—recall subtle memories, perform complex calculations in milliseconds, and even rewire itself in some cases. Yet despite this, it is still an imperfect piece of meat. If you think that its [creation] is evidence of God, then I'd argue you certainly don't think God does a very good job…

I am overawed with the way my brain works. I am amazed at how I can travel back through my memories and relive my experiences. I am amazed at how my brain can manifest creativity, ingenuity, initiative, insight, discretion, and a mass of deep emotions. My brain, which is just an average brain, is infinitely more complex than the most sophisticated of computers. However, the above atheist sees his as "an imperfect piece of meat." Something therefore is wrong with it. It's not working properly. Of course, I wouldn't say that God didn't do a very good job of creating it, but I would rather say that the professing atheist isn't using it properly. It's just meat because he isn't using that life-giving stimulant of "common sense."

When a brain is hard-wired to the power of common sense, the eyes will marvel at the genius of God's unspeakably creative hand. The eyes will look around at the incredibly colorful flowers, the thousands of amazing birds, the massive trees, the tasty fruits, the life-giving sun, the moon, and the innumerable stars. Yes, something *is* terribly wrong with a brain that refuses common sense…and even these few thoughts will make no sense to a brain that lacks common sense.

Let's take a look at your list of "evidence." Creation proves there's a creator. It most certainly does not. Even calling it "Creation" shows your considerable bias. This is pure assertion. There are far better theories out there than "Goddidit" that are actually consistent with how the universe is. This does not mean that God does not exist but it far from means God must exist.

It's not easy to be an atheist. He has to deny both common reason and logic. But, it seems worth it to some, because they think you then become a moral free agent. However, you can look at the miracle of creation and deny the genius of the Creator, but He still exists. You can call Him an "imaginary friend," but He still exists and sees everything you do and even what you think. You can call any reference to the Bible "circular reasoning," but that Word will judge you on Judgment Day whether you believe it or not.

> **The Asunist Headquarters**
>
> A group known as "asunists" has produced a manifesto explaining why they believe that the sun doesn't exist:
>
> 1. An entire desert tribe of men, women, and children was once killed by the sun. Therefore the sun doesn't exist.
>
> 2. Intelligent scientists have searched the night sky for the sun, and found no evidence for its existence.
>
> 3. They also entered a pitch-black room and studied a book about the sun. Again, they found no empirical evidence.
>
> 4. Beliefs were confirmed by interviewing members of the Braille Institute.
>
> 5. The millions who testified that they have seen a brilliant ball of fire in the sky are unscientific dimwitted liars. The asunists continue to hold their meetings in a dark room and tell each other that it is intelligent to believe that the sun doesn't exist.

Staunch evolutionists believe the theory as though their life depended on it. They treat every find as the Gospel truth. They so believe in it they would perhaps put their hand on a Bible and swear it was "the truth, the whole truth, and nothing but the truth, so help me God." Maybe not. Why the passion? Because their lives *do* depend on it.

If your deity can have always existed, the universe can have as well.

To deal with the dilemma of God and His eternal nature, atheists will often abandon their own accepted science and create the straw man of an eternal universe. Stephen Hawking said:

> This argument about whether or not the universe had a beginning persisted into the nineteenth and twentieth centuries. It was conducted mainly on the basis of theology and philosophy, with little consideration of observational evidence. This may have been reasonable, given the notoriously unreliable character of cosmological observations, until fairly recently. The cosmologist Sir Arthur Eddington once said, "Don't worry if your theory doesn't agree with the observations, because they are probably wrong." But if your theory disagrees with the Second Law of Thermodynamics, it is in bad trouble. In fact, the theory that the universe has existed forever is in serious difficulty with the Second Law of Thermodynamics. The Second Law states that disorder always increases with time. Like the argument about human progress, it indicates that there must have been a beginning. Otherwise, the universe would be in a state of complete disorder by now, and everything would be at the same temperature.[3]

In other words, everything material degenerates (rots). An apple rots in time. So does an egg. Rocks crumble into dust, in time. If the universe was around forever (trillions and trillions plus years), everything material would have turned to dust.

However, the Bible teaches that God is not material. He is what Scripture calls "spirit" (see John 4:24). He is the essence of life itself, the creator of human life, and is invisible (as is "life"), immortal (not touched by death), and eternal (no beginning or end).

All who are "born" of His Spirit (see John 3:1-5) receive the gift of eternal life (see Romans 6:23). They are sealed with the spirit of life. If you find all this hard to believe, simply repent and trust Jesus Christ (surrender to His Lordship), and you will know the truth, and the truth will make you free (see John 8:31-32).

Ray, do you call everyone who disagrees with you and posts a comment here an atheist? That's a bit much. There could be quite a few individuals here who just want to set you straight on topics like evolution. Which does not make them atheists. I accept evolution and I believe in God and I am not alone. I for one would just like to see you open your mind and read some peer reviewed articles on the subject and try learn something instead of maligning science and spewing ignorance.

There is only one God and He revealed Himself and how we were created through His Word. In Scripture we are told that God made man in His own image. He created Adam as a man and then He created a female for him to reproduce, after his own kind.

So the god (evolution) you believe in is what is known as an "idol." An idol is a creation of the human mind and is often shaped by hands with wood or stone. The reason we are so prone to idolatry is that an idol doesn't tell us what to do. An idol doesn't consider lust to be adultery and hatred to be murder, or condemn lying and stealing. An idol is dumb, and the Bible says those who create them are like them. We can shape our little god into anything we feel comfortable with, even if it's an unscientific theory that we believe gives us a license to sin.

You are right about not being alone when it comes to idolatry. Millions worship false gods. You may not have formed your own religion with your god (Hinduism has 450 million gods), but he is extremely popular, especially in the Western world and among university students. And anyone who is gullible enough to believe in evolution will also be gullible enough to believe that when they create a god in their mind, it somehow does exist. Yet it doesn't. It's a figment of a fertile imagination (the place of imagery). Idolaters still have to face the God of the Bible on the Day of Judgment, whether they believe in Him or not. Imagine that—standing alone before the throne of a holy and perfect Creator, the One that spoke the sun into existence and has seen every thought that has passed through your sinful mind. Imagine that—standing alone before Almighty God who requires an account of every idle word you have spoken, and every deed you have done, even if it is in secret.

The smartest man alive (Stephen Hawking) is an atheist. You think him a fool because he does not believe in your vile Bronze Age superstitions.

Not so. Stephen Hawking isn't a fool. He believes in God. Look at what he said about Him: "It would be very difficult to explain why the universe should have begun in just this way, except as the act of a God who intended to create beings like us."[4]

He also said, "The odds against a universe like ours coming out of something like the Big Bang are enormous. I think there are clearly religious implications…"[5]

It doesn't take a rocket scientist to look at this amazing creation and see the genius of the Creator. A child can know that. Your stumbling block isn't intellectual as you maintain…it's moral.

Atheists don't hate any god, fairy, leprechaun, unicorn, or other fictional being. It's impossible to hate something that does not exist…

That's right. Atheists don't hate fairies, leprechauns, or unicorns, because they don't exist. It is impossible to hate something that doesn't exist. And that makes the point. Atheists—like the painting experts hated the painter—hate God because He *does* exist. Many atheists spend time thinking about God, then arguing about Him, then blaspheming His name (what greater hatred can you have for a person than to use their name as a cuss word?), and showing contempt for and ridicule of those that love Him.

Atheists have the axiomatic evidence of creation and of their consciences, and are therefore without excuse. By professing the blindness of atheism they deny the God-given light that He has given each of us.

There are some cultures in which people show so much contempt for a family member that has wronged them they actually deny his existence. They refuse to acknowledge that he existed as a son. They don't want to see him, hear from him, or talk to him. That's what the professing atheist does with God, and his or her reason for doing so is moral. It's not intellectual. If it was an intellectual issue there wouldn't be any argument. But through their moral conscience atheists know that God requires an account for every action and every word (including our thought life); they can't stand that thought, and so they deny His existence.

Ray, I have a question for you. I am getting frustrated having to try and "prove" God's existence day in and day out to unbelievers all the time. Do I really need to "prove" God to anyone or just preach the Gospel? I don't see why I should have to "prove" what God has already said in His Word. I'd love some advice on how you handle this.

We don't have to prove that God exists to the professing atheist. This is because he intuitively knows that He exists. Every person has a God-given conscience. The Bible tells us that this is the "work of the law written on their hearts." Just as every sane human being knows that it's wrong to lie, steal, kill, and commit adultery, he knows that God should be first in his life.

The professing atheist not only has the testimony of his impartial conscience, but he also has the testimony of creation. It "declares" the glory of God, and the person who denies the voice of conscience and the voice of creation is without excuse. If death seizes upon him and he is still in his sins, he will face the wrath of a holy Creator, whether he believes in Him or not.

This is why I don't spend too much time trying to convince anyone that there is a God. To do so is to waste time and energy. Sinners don't need convincing that God exists; they need convincing that *sin* exists and that they are in terrible danger. The only biblical way to do this is to go through the moral Law and explain that God considers lust to be adultery and hatred to be murder, etc. It is the revelation that God is holy and just and sees our thought life that convinces us that we are in danger of eternal damnation. That's what sent me to the Cross for mercy and that's what sinners need to hear. So never be discouraged from preaching the Gospel, and don't get sidetracked by the rabbit trails of issues that don't really matter.

FAITH AND SCIENCE

To attempt to use faith in science, or science in faith, simply demeans them both.

9

Not so. Every scientific experiment is done "in faith." If a scientist had the results in front of him where he could see them, why would he experiment? He conducts a test because he doesn't yet see the results.

Edison kept experimenting with the light bulb over and over because he believed he would eventually see the light. It was because of his faith that he got a result. He believed without seeing, until the light gave him that for which he was looking. Never make the mistake of believing you can ever remove faith from that equation.

No doubt there is something behind disdain for "faith." Is it because it has the connotation that God is somehow in the mix? That would be another mistake. As Albert Einstein famously and rightly said, "Science without religion is lame, religion without science is blind."

Although Edison wasn't a believer (he's one of my great heroes), it was God who gave him light. Without his God-given, wonderfully inventive brain, we would probably still be in darkness.

It's also important to understand that "religion" (for want of a better word) is not "blind" faith. God has given us all the evidence we need, including "many infallible proofs," and He exhorts us to "come, let us reason together."

The fact that some don't recognize the evidence doesn't mean it's not there. Would we still consider Edison a genius if the light came on, but he refused to see it? He would either be blind or a fool.

God has given light to every man (see John 1:9)—through this wonderful creation, through the undeniable voice of the conscience, and through plain old common sense.

When the Bible speaks of "faith" in God, that is not a reference to an intellectual acknowledgment that He exists (we all know that). It's speaking of an implicit *trust* in His person and His promises.

Discoveries about the natural world, especially an alien planet, should amaze everyone. The religious can be amazed at how God decided to put the universe together. The non-religious can share in the awe of the natural world, with the promise of more discoveries around the corner. It's sad, Ray, that you don't have this feeling of awe…

I would be grateful not to be called "religious." If you are a little confused as to why most Christians don't like being called that, let me give you a comparison that you may think is extreme, but as far as I am concerned, it's not. It's like the difference between "African American" and the "n" word. One is culturally acceptable. The other has extremely negative connotations.

I want to distance myself from the hypocrisy, the greed, the pedophilia, and the dead tradition of religion. Marx rightly called it the "opiate of the masses." I don't want a *religion*. I want a *relationship* with my Creator.

The feeling of awe that you get at the promise of new discoveries is a tiny part of what Christians feel in knowing God. You get a sense of awe because you *see* the creation. We are overawed beyond words because we *know* the Creator. I would like to be able to give you another comparison between those two experiences, but I can't think of any because they are so far apart.

When I look at the magnificence of the Grand Canyon, or the incredible power of Niagara Falls, or the sun, the stars, birds, flowers, elephants, lions, etc.—all of this amazing creation—I don't just see the creation, I see the wonder, the glory, and the power of the Creator.

I haven't always seen this way. I used to think that I could see, but I was blind until I came to know Him who said, "I am the light of the world. He who follows Me shall not walk in darkness, but have the light of life" (John 8:12).

Consider what the Bible says about praising God's creation and ignoring the Creator:

> [W]hen they knew and recognized Him as God, they did not honor and glorify Him as God or give Him thanks. But instead they became futile and godless in their thinking [with vain imaginings, foolish reasoning, and stupid speculations] and their senseless minds were darkened (Romans 1:21, *Amplified Bible*).

How many things have we discovered recently (within the last one hundred years)? Microwaves, TV, lasers, flight, radio, electricity, cars, computers, the Internet, new species, etc. I could go on and on about what we have recently discovered. Just because we don't know something doesn't mean it isn't true. (I know that last statement can go both ways!) When Galileo said the Earth rotated around the Sun, he was put under house arrest by the church because they "knew" the Sun rotated around the Earth. How did they know this? They got their information from the Bible. What will we "know" in the next one hundred years?

Please study your history. It was the Roman Catholic Church (not the Christian Church) that arrested Galileo. I have spoken to hundreds of Roman Catholics, and when you ask them, "Are you a Christian?" most say, "No. I'm a Roman Catholic." They know the difference. Catholics are steeped in tradition, and Christians adhere only to the Bible. And the Catholic Church didn't get their information "from the Bible" (it was a banned Book).

Skeptics of Christianity often try to demean Scripture by saying that the Christian Church persecuted Galileo when he maintained that the Earth circled the Sun. As a professor of astronomy at the University of Pisa, Galileo was required to teach the accepted theory of his time that the Sun and all the planets revolved around the Earth. Later at the University of Padua he was exposed to a new theory, proposed by Nicolaus Copernicus, that the Earth and all the other planets revolved around the Sun. Galileo's observations with his new telescope convinced him of the truth of Copernicus's sun-centered or heliocentric theory.

Galileo's support for the heliocentric theory got him into trouble with the Roman Catholic Church. In 1633, during the Inquisition, he was convicted of heresy and ordered to recant (publicly withdraw) his support of Copernicus. The Roman Catholic Church sentenced him to life imprisonment, but his advanced age allowed him to serve the term under house arrest at his villa outside of Florence, Italy. The Christian Church therefore should not be blamed for his imprisonment. It was the Roman Catholic Church that persecuted Galileo.

> Under the sentence of imprisonment Galileo remained till his death in 1642. It is, however, untrue to speak of him as in any proper sense a "prisoner." As his Protestant biographer, von Gebler, tells us, "One glance at the truest historical source for the famous trial would convince anyone that Galileo spent altogether twenty-two days in the buildings of the Holy Office [during the Inquisition], and even then not in a prison cell with barred

windows, but in the handsome and commodious apartment of an
official of the Inquisition" (*Catholic Encyclopedia*).

Also, when you speak of how many things "we discovered" in the
last one hundred years, I hope you keep in mind that man simply
uncovers hidden laws that allow him to invent things. We would have
no microwaves without the already existing electromagnetic waves.
There would be no television without the laws that govern television
waves, and radio communication without radio waves, etc. We
couldn't fly if the law of aerodynamics didn't already exist, or use any
electrical appliance without the existing laws that govern electricity.
All these things were around before we "discovered" them. Science
merely uncovers what God has already made.

Could you tell me how old you believe the Earth to be, and why?

I have no idea how old the Earth is, but I'm not alone in this.
Science can't make up its mind either. Just over one hundred years
ago, scientists thought that the Earth was about 100 million years old.
Soon after, they changed their minds and came to the confident belief
that the correct number was 500 million years. Then they changed
their minds again and the figure jumped to 1.3 billion years. It wasn't
long until they did a double take on that one and said that they
believed it was perhaps 3 billion years old. Of course, now they think
that it may be 4.55 billion years old, give or take a billion years.

I'm sure that contemporary scientists think they have the
right number this time, until they change their minds again when
more data comes along…and, of course, none of the "faithful"
will question it.

*This is all very confusing; can you please explain why scientists cannot
make absolute claims, but at the same time they are not allowed to improve
a theory or something like the age of the Earth, while at the same time you
are allowed to make absolute claims about God, sinning, and the Bible?*

Science admits that it cannot know anything for certain. It's
forever discovering more knowledge and therefore changing its
beliefs. That's not something I made up. It's a fact. This is because

science doesn't have all the facts. Only God does. He is omniscient. None of us can get a mental grip of what omniscience is because it is too much for our minds.

I assume that you are an atheist, so you will have to be patient with me for a moment as I talk about a realm in which you don't believe.

God exists whether we believe He does or not. He is omnipotent (can do anything), omnipresent (dwells everywhere), and He is of course omniscient (He knows everything). That means that nothing is hidden from His eyes. Think of a number. Think of a color. Are they in your mind? Don't tell anyone. Only you and God know what they are. He sees everything that enters your mind. After all, He made your amazing brain and gave you the ability to think.

Now, in your mind, travel to Mars. Okay, dig down a thousand miles into the dirt until you find a large rock. Crack it open. Grab an electron microscope and study it closely. Then magnify the image a million times until you can see the atoms. You are the second person to see them. God was already there. He knows and sees what He has made. Everything. All at once.

He sees every thought of every human being in history—not one at a time. All at once. And He's not confused. You and I struggle to entertain two thoughts at once, but God has all knowledge.

So when we speak of absolutes, we are speaking of a different realm. Man is limited. God is not. In addition to having absolute knowledge, He is absolute perfection and absolute righteousness. And because of what He is, He makes absolute claims about right and wrong. This is what the Bible says of God's omniscience and omnipresence:

> Lord, you have searched me [thoroughly] and have known me. You know my downsitting and my uprising; You understand my thought afar off. You sift and search out my path and my lying down, and You are acquainted with all my ways. For there is not a word in my tongue [still unuttered], but, behold, O Lord, You know it altogether. You have beset me and shut me in— behind and before, and You have laid Your hand upon me. Your [infinite] knowledge is too wonderful for me; it is high above me, I cannot reach it. Where could I go from Your Spirit? Or where could I flee from Your presence? If I ascend up into

heaven, You are there; if I make my bed in Sheol (the place of the dead), behold, You are there (Psalm 139:1-8, *Amplified Bible*).

If all this is true, it is unspeakably consoling for the Christian, and extremely frightening for the atheist (the "unbeliever"). Fortunately, there is a way to find out if it is true. God is there in the room with you right now…He's seen everything you have done (even if it was done in complete darkness). He has been a witness to everything you have thought, and you have greatly angered Him—whether you believe it or not. So, today, repent of your sins and trust the Savior, and you will come to know Him. Absolutely.

So what is the point of your criticism of science? That because creationism is useless, it cannot be used to commit genocide or pollute the planet, and therefore ought to be preferred to mainstream science?

We unquestionably live in a world of insanity where genocide and pollution occur, where it has become commonplace for fathers to murder their children, husbands to beat their wives, kids to kill kids at school. It is an insane world where people breathe in carcinogens in the form of a cigarette to feel cool, where it's normal and good to poison yourself through alcoholic intoxication, where lying and stealing is acceptable behavior.

We live in a world where mothers kill their children before they are born, where priests in the name of God molest children, where so-called rational people believe that we are related to primates and call such unfounded imaginations "science."

The Bible reveals the root cause of all this mess. The issue has nothing to do with science or even with creationism, really. The issue is a corruption that the Bible calls "sin." The essence of sin is rebellion against our Creator. It's an evil that dwells within each of us, refusing to yield to His moral government. We are like rebels who hijack a plane that we have no idea how to fly.

We are plummeting toward the ground with no hope of salvation, and yet the Control Tower offers to guide us to safety. That's the core of conversion—a total yielding of the controls back to the lawful Owner.

We justly deserve death. God offers us everlasting life. Please, repent today. Apologize to God for your transgressions of His Law. Think about your sins, then think about the Savior. Think about what He did for you on the Cross. Trust Jesus Christ—give Him total control, and you will have the ultimate promise from God "who cannot lie." He will save you from death.

THE CASE AGAINST EVOLUTION

The first, and main, problem is the very existence of the Big Bang. One may wonder, what came before? If space-time did not exist then, how could everything appear from nothing? What arose first? The universe or the laws determining its evolution? Explaining this initial singularity— where and when it all began—still remains the most intractable problem of modern cosmology.

Searching for answers, scientists recently announced that they may have the puzzle pieces to the fundamental mystery of the universe. Using a NASA telescope, they think they've figured out the cosmic question of where we came from. Their conclusion? According to Ciska Markwick-Kemper of the University of Manchester in England, "In the end, everything comes from space dust."[6] She and her fellow astronomers believe that space dust was "belched from dying stars" about 8 billion light years away.[7]

The dilemma is that no matter how far away or how long ago scientists estimate the very first dust particle came into being, the logical question remains: *Where did that dust come from?*

It's unavoidable—at some point, you're forced to conclude that there must be an uncaused cause (a "First Cause") that brought everything else into being. This conclusion agrees with logic, reason, and scientific laws. In all of history, there has never been an instance of anything spontaneously appearing out of nowhere. Something being created from nothing is contrary to all known science.

In short, the evolutionary view cannot offer a logical, scientific explanation for either the origin or the complexity of the universe. There are only two choices: Either no one created everything out of

CREATION MUST HAVE A CREATOR

nothing, or Someone—an intelligent, omnipotent, eternal First Cause—created everything out of nothing. Which makes more sense?[8]

We are animals. If you deny that we are, then you need to go take a basic science course.

This reveals why believers in the theory of evolution have the convictions of religious zealots. It also reveals why those who don't believe as they do are seen as ignorant knuckle-draggers. If evolution is true, then man is simply an animal. That means he is free to embark on his sexual prowls, because it is nothing but a basic instinct to do so. It's his procreative nature to fornicate, and therefore not a sin. For the atheist, this is a hill to die on.

As one visitor to my blog said:

> We are humans, yes, we are apes too. What you seem to ignore is that classifications need levels of categories. For instance, chimps are chimps, just like humans are humans, and we both are apes (higher order of classification). The ape equation, we being animals too, is a natural conclusion, nothing to do with being "sinners."

Evolution swings open a door to do whatever the evolutionist pleases, as long as what he does is within the bounds of a civil law he is ever expanding to accommodate his sinful desires.

If man is an animal, he can even justify homosexuality and bestiality because "other" animals do it. To him, evolution is a license to act like an animal, and he does.

The dictionary says that an animal is "any such living thing other than a human being." The word *human* means "lowly" or "frail," and the word *being* means that we are aware of our existence. We are unique among God's creation in that we are not only morally responsible, but we are aware that we are going to die. There is a basic instinct within all sane human beings that wants to live. So, let me concede slightly and let you call it "an animal instinct." Now, obey your basic instinct—turn from your sins, trust in Jesus Christ, and God will make you fit to survive on the Day of Judgment.

We are apes. If there is such thing as a God, and if such God made us to His image, well, he obviously made the other apes to His image, too.

God *did* make man in His image, and He made male and female so that they could reproduce after their own kind. Evolution believers erroneously believe that all creatures (millions of kinds), *by themselves*, came into being as male and female, and then gave themselves the ability to reproduce after their own kind.

The difference between man and apes is that man is a moral being. If you don't believe it, read the comments on my blog and see how moral atheists point to the moral Law to say that I have deviated morally from the truth (see Exodus 20:16).

What's more, God made man as a man. He created sheep as they are; as sheep. He created birds and fish—as they are—birds and fish. They were "in the beginning" as they are now. Nothing evolved and nothing is evolving. Tadpoles still change into frogs and caterpillars still change into butterflies, and they do that

---

Man or Mouse?

Have you ever wondered why scientists do research with mice? I thought about it recently when I heard Mr. Ronald Evans, Ph.D., from the "Salk Institute for Biological Studies" say, "All of the genetic components are exactly the same in mice as in people." Wow. All the genetic components are there. This opens up a whole new realm for the imagination of the believer in the theory of evolution. Man may have evolved from the mouse, or should I say, had a common ancestor as the mouse.

For an evolutionist it really is just common sense when you think of the homologous structure of the mouse. Think of how the mouse uses its human-like hands in a human-like manner. Think of its human-like ears, human-like eyes, mouth, and teeth (kind of). The mouse, as do humans, has a heart, brain, liver, kidneys, lungs, legs, feet, blood, veins, etc. Humans and mice both need male and female to survive. But more: "As fellow mammals, humans share many physiological, anatomical, and metabolic parallels with mice" (Nadeau and Taylor, "Lengths of chromosomal segments conserved since divergence of man and mouse," *Proc. Natl. Acad. Sci.* 81:814-818, 1984).

So there you have it—a new theory for naïve believers to blindly embrace…and why not? There are no rules and no bounds of the imagination when it comes to the theory tale of evolution.

There is one similarity I forgot to mention. Both the mouse and the human being are easily trapped and killed. One by the smell of cheese, the other by a mere hint of sin.

because God made them that way, not because of evolution.

Ah, now I am experiencing nostalgia for my college days. I lived in a women's dorm, and just about every night there would be about a dozen people sitting together in the hall, studying or discussing Serious Ideas…while brushing each other's hair. I don't know if the thought occurred to me at the time, but looking back…wow, we were a bunch of primates. Human social behavior is so very similar to great ape social behavior. You have to wonder how some people fail to make the connection.

Actually, we *do* have a lot in common with primates. We both eat, sleep, drink, have eyes, a nose, a mouth, two ears, a face, teeth, a stomach, liver, kidneys, blood, lungs, and a brain. However, pigs also eat, sleep, drink, have eyes, a nose, a mouth, two ears, a face, teeth, a stomach, liver, kidneys, blood, lungs, and a brain. Come to think of it, I have seen people eat like pigs (especially at all-you-can-eat buffets), and I have to admit I have been known to sound like one when I sleep.

If you need a skin transplant, you may get pig skin, because that is the closest skin to *Homo sapiens*. Pig tissue is very close to human skin tissue (they are even similar in color). That's why organs from pigs may be used in transplant cases without rejection (to some degree). The muscle fibers and arrangements are very similar in pigs and humans.

Dogs also eat, sleep, drink, have eyes, a nose, a mouth, two ears, a face, teeth, a stomach, liver, kidneys, blood, lungs, and a brain. They are extremely social animals, appreciate company, communicate with each other, guard their home territory, and play with Frisbees. Some twisted folks even try to justify homosexuality by comparing their behavior to the disgusting behavior of dogs.

So, were our ancestors apes, pigs, or dogs? That's up to you and your imagination, if you believe in evolution.

Name one feature about humanity that can be demonstrated as unique.

Atheism. Only human beings have the ability to bow the knee and worship the God that gave them life. Only human beings have the ability to deny His evident existence. We are utterly unique among God's creation because He has made us in His image.

So what was Darwin's stance on racism? [He was] pretty much against it. Especially if you take into account his historical and cultural context, which you guys like forgetting when attacking his character...I also think racism is stupid.

Darwin was nothing but a blatant racist, a bigot of a man, who held to the belief that black people are inferior to whites. This is what he said:

> At some future period not very distant as measured by centuries, the civilized races of man will almost certainly exterminate and replace the savage races throughout the world. At the same time the anthropomorphous apes...will no doubt be exterminated. The break between man and his nearest Allies will then be wider, for it will intervene between man in a more civilized state, as we may hope, even than the Caucasian, and some ape as low as the baboon, instead of as now between the Negro or Australian and the gorilla.[9]

Read it again slowly and make a note of the comparison between black people and gorillas. Darwin's white robe is stained with bigotry, and his clan rallies to his godless cause with religious zeal. Watch his hooded believers (those who hide behind Internet unanimity) give a fiery defense of Darwin's evil racist beliefs.

One more thing: Look at the questioner's statement that "I also think racism is stupid." It reveals something about his character. I suppose he thinks rape and pedophilia are also stupid. Yet those behaviors are to be expected from those who deny that there is good and evil.

Life forms change over time and given enough time, they can—and did— change dramatically. GET OVER IT! No one is ever, ever going to go back to the idea that species were created fully developed at a specific point in time. NEVER. The details of the theory may change but not the framework. There is no faith involved. Move on. Evolution happens.

You have said, "Life forms change over time and given enough time, they can—and did—change dramatically." This is what you believe. It's a statement that is based on faith. You weren't there when the life forms were created, and you didn't see them change. You don't know how life began; you simply believe that what you have been told happened actually did happen. Like it or not, you are a "believer" in the theory of evolution.

If you have faith in ever-changing science, you can't "know" anything for certain. You have to *trust* that what you believe is the truth, because science is forever gaining new knowledge and upgrading its beliefs. What you believe to be true today may be laughed at in one hundred years' time. That's the truth. History attests to it.

Faith is often shunned by atheists and skeptics, because the word has "religious" overtones: "Faith is a cop-out. It is intellectual bankruptcy. If the only way you can accept an assertion is by faith, then you are conceding that it can't be taken on its own merits."[10]

Of course, the Christian lives by faith also. We weren't there "in the beginning" when God created the heavens and the earth. But our trust is in Him who is utterly faithful (trustworthy), unchanging (unlike science), and infallible. That's the big difference.

Could an evolutionist give you any evidence that would make you believe in it?

Could I give you any evidence that would make you believe in fairies or that the sun is made of ice? Even answering that question would reveal something about you intellectually. However, your question is even more loaded, because it carries with it a subtle implication.

Being a Christian means that I know God. I don't know "about" Him; I *know* Him. That's the biblical definition of a Christian— someone who knows the Lord (see John 17:3). This isn't bigotry or arrogance. That's just the way it is.

God's Word tells me that He created man in His own image, morally cognizant, and as male and female. To believe in a theory that says otherwise is to call God a liar. This is something I would never do, in light of the irrefutable evidence of His proven reality. It would be far easier for me to believe in fairies and that the sun is made of ice, than to believe in the imaginations of Darwinian evolutionists.

I've been looking into the issue for more than thirty years, and I have never seen a hint of genuine evidence of species-to-species transitional forms in the fossil record. The theory stands or falls on the supposed links between species. Even if you came up with what you believe is evidence, time would prove it to be another hoax, as it has so often in the past.

So you are flogging a decomposed horse. You have been duped. Evolution isn't true. It never has been and it never will be, no matter how long you wait for evidence. That is upsetting for its true believers, because it leaves only one alternative—that God created mankind as male and female and that you and I are morally responsible to Him.

However, if you really want the truth—if you are open to genuine evidence—simply believe the words of the infallible Creator rather than the words of fallible man: "Then Jesus said to those Jews who believed in Him, 'If you abide in My word, you are My disciples indeed. And you shall know the truth, and the truth shall make you free'" (John 8:31-32).

Using your thirty years of in-depth research into the evidence for evolution, please inform [us] why Tiktaalik doesn't count as a transitional form.

Let's look closely at Tiktaalik, which evolutionists believe is an example of a species-to-species transitional form. We will go to the experts at Berkley. In an article published back in May of 2006, they ask the question, "What has the head of a crocodile and the gills of a fish?" (Wait a minute. Are the experts saying they have found a "Crocafish"? Why then am I so mocked by evolutionists when I ask you to show me a "Crocaduck"?[11])

This is their fishy story: "Unearthed in Arctic Canada by a team of researchers led by Neil Shubin, Edward Daeschler, and Farish Jenkins, Tiktaalik is technically a fish, complete with scales and gills—but it has the flattened head of a crocodile and unusual fins."[12]

So this find is "technically a fish, complete with scales and gills." Let me repeat what the experts said, in case you missed it. Tiktaalik "is technically a fish, complete with scales and gills," and it has an unusual head that looks like a crocodile. Big deal. This has nothing at all to do with the theory of evolution or species-to-species transitional forms. It's a fish, and God has created thousands of other fish with strange heads.

I can hardly believe how people will swallow anything as long as it has a big (or strange) name and is believed to be millions of years old. I wonder why atheists are the ultimate skeptics when it comes to the axiom of God, and blind believers when it comes to the theory tale of evolution.

Here's a question for you — if a "missing link" was discovered, or something showing that men and apes had a common ancestor, would you stop believing in God?

To answer this question I'm going to have to use an "ATMAM." "ATMAM" is an acronym for an "Analogy That Makes Atheists Mad." Here goes: The question is similar to asking me, "If you discovered that your mother-in-law was a draught horse, would you stop believing that your wife existed?" The analogy is applicable because I know that it's impossible for Sue's mother to be another species (it's against nature), and I could never deny the existence of my wife because I know her. Atheists think that a "Christian" is someone who "believes" that God exists. That's not true. A Christian (in the biblical sense) is someone who "knows" God experientially. This fact is almost impossible to get through to an atheist, but I will repeat it from another angle. I believed in God's existence before I was a Christian. I wasn't dim-witted enough to look at creation and say that there is no Creator. Of course I believed in God like every other sane and reasoning human being. But on the 25th of April, 1972, at 1:30 in the morning, I came to know the Lord. I moved out of the realm of belief into the realm of experience. I know Him "Whom to know is life eternal." When a sinner comes to know God it's called "conversion," or "the new birth" (see John 3:3).

Michael Shermer was raised in a fundamentalist Christian home. He presumably came home one day and told his parents something like this: "Mom and Dad, I've been studying biology in college and you know what you and Pastor Bob taught about how everything was created all at once? Well, as it turns out, there's a couple of centuries' worth of evidence to show that it didn't happen that way." If you were in their place, what would you say to your kid? (Michael Shermer is the publisher of Skeptic *magazine.)*

Michael, your parents and pastor may have encouraged you to give your heart to Jesus when you were a little boy. It is wrong to do that. That is the recipe for a false conversion. They instead should have taught you the Ten Commandments—that God considers lust to be adultery, and hatred to be murder; that lying lips are an abomination to the Lord. Then the fact that Jesus paid your fine—by suffering for your sins to save you from hell—would have made sense to you. You need to repent and trust the Savior to escape God's eternal justice. When you do that, you will come to know God. Not know "about" Him, but you will know Him personally. He will transform your life and grant you the gift of everlasting life. John 14:21 is either true or it isn't: "He who has My commandments and keeps them, it is he who loves Me. And he who loves Me will be loved by My Father, and I will love him and manifest Myself to him." As you obey Him, His presence will become more real to you than the early morning sunlight.

A theory exists out there that contradicts God's Word. It says that man wasn't made in God's image, but that we evolved, over a long period of time, from primates. If I were your parent, I would say that when you are told this, I want you to ask questions about it. I want you to be the ultimate skeptic. Don't just believe it. The entire theory stands or falls on whether or not there is proof. So ask for scientific proof.

Evolutionists say that all the animals we have now were not as we see them. They were radically different. Dinosaurs, over millions of years, became birds, fish became lizards, dogs were something else, primates evolved into human beings, etc. So, when they tell you this, ask why there are no species-to-species transitional forms in the fossil record. Why is there no evidence anywhere (in the billions of bones of dead animals) of any species becoming another species?

When they maintain that there are masses of fossils that prove this, don't take their word for it. Press the issue. Blind faith is another word for ignorance. Say you want facts. Ask for specific scientific evidence of species-to-species transitional forms in the fossil record. When they say that museums are full of them, don't just believe it as they do. Press the issue again. They will talk about variation (evolution) between species. That's not Darwinian evolution. It's a rabbit trail. Ask again for just one example of species-to-species evolution.

They will try to sidetrack you by talking about moths being stuck to trees, vestigial organs, mutations, bipedalism, or mitochondrial DNA. Or they will maintain that there is something called "observed speciation," or try to dazzle you with names like Sinosauropteryx and Ambulocetur and other pseudo-intellectualisms. Then they will say that they aren't experts, and use words like "maybe," "possibly," "perhaps," "probably." When they say that science has the proof somewhere, push it. Demand evidence like your life depended on it. Tell them that you want to use your God-given brain to make a rational decision regarding evolution. You want to know if it's true. Stay open-minded. If it is true, then embrace it. If it's not, reject it.

If they maintain that there's just a "handful" of bones to prove it, don't believe them. There are none. They don't have any evidence anywhere for their theory. None. It's all blind faith, conjecture, and wild imagination.

So, Michael, you will have a choice between the two beliefs of the origin of mankind. There is no fence to sit on. Was it evolution or were we intelligently designed by God? You can either rest in the evidence of the God you know personally, or you can turn your back on Him (and His gift of everlasting life), and blindly have faith in an unscientific theory. And why would an intelligent person do that?

Cosmological evolution is not the same as Darwin's theory of organic evolution. How many times would you say you've been corrected about that? Seriously—how many times, approximately? Just ten times? A hundred? A thousand times? And still you repeat it!

The evolutionist says, "Let's have a debate about the validity of Darwinian evolution," and when he finds himself in a corner with no species-to-species transitional forms in the fossil record, he changes the subject of the debate. Suddenly, it's not Darwinian evolution, but "cosmological" evolution. But I'm staying with the subject.

You have faith in an unscientific theory (Darwinian evolution) that is in great error, and one which cannot be supported with anything but conjecture. Evolution is nothing but a long and winding rabbit trail that leads nowhere. You have no explanation as to the origin of creation (how it began), why it began, or where the materials came from for the beginning. It is a senseless theory, and only the gullible believe. Evolutionists are as gullible as those who see the face of Mary in a tree knot or a piece of pizza.

All forms of evolution are a non-issue when compared to your eternal salvation. So set it aside for a moment and think about where you will spend eternity. Think about this precious gift of life. Think about your mortality. Think about your sins, and then think about what God did on the Cross to save you from their eternal consequences.

Evolution is responsible for life's diversity, not for gravity. You are a bit misinformed. "Gravity" is in the "physics" section. "Evolution" can be found in the "biology" section.

If (as is commonly accepted) the natural phenomenon of evolution had no end in mind when it created all living things, it is incredibly intelligent, but it forgot that they would go spinning into space without the law of gravity. So it was fortunate for us that gravity just happened to be around to stop that disaster.

Where did gravity then come from? If evolution had nothing to do with it, who or what created it? "Chance" or "accident" is too big a leap of blind faith for me. The evolutionist's version of "just believe" isn't good enough. I want verifiable scientific facts.

And while we are looking for facts, explain to me where the other laws that govern the universe came from, e.g., the laws of thermodynamics, of motion, and the laws of heat. Why don't we see chaos everywhere instead of order?

CREATION MUST HAVE A CREATOR

Of course your "scientific" answer will be, "We don't yet know where they came from, but one thing we are sure of, God didn't create them."

Newton's discovery of the law of gravitation showed science that the gravitational constant is in direct proportion to the product of the masses divided by the square of the distance apart. However, that doesn't explain the nature of gravity. Despite its mystery, the brilliant Newton attributed its origin to the genius of Almighty God. So do I.

MacArthur says, "The most damaging ideologies of the nineteenth and twentieth centuries were all rooted in Darwinism." So what he is saying is that we would be better off if scientific advancements never happened. That is totally bogus.

Genuine scientific advancement is wonderful. However, Darwinism is not scientific. It is a brainless and unproven theory that comes from the imaginations of sinful men. I was once a believer, until I looked for empirical evidence. It just isn't there.

The irony is that anyone who denies the mindless theory is considered to be an unscientific moron, when the truth is any evolutionary believer (especially an atheist) speaking on behalf of science is like Jeffery Dahmer speaking on behalf of the Boy Scouts of America.

What a liar! Are you capable of honesty when it comes to science? Ray, what is the intelligent design in fish that live in caves and produce non-functional eyes? What about the intelligent design in the coronary artery? We have one artery to supply the heart with oxygen…one artery. If this one vessel gets clogged…coronary. Intelligent design adds redundancies, especially on vital parts to prevent the machine from breaking down. You are telling me that this is the best that Jesus could do?

It seems obvious to me that fish that live in dark caves under the water don't need functioning eyes because it's dark down there. Regarding your clogged arteries problem—lay off the double-double cheeseburgers, the cigarettes, and the alcohol, get plenty of exercise, and you won't clog up your coronary artery. Then you can die healthy.

You should also remember that you have been designed with only one esophagus. I wouldn't clog that up either. Same with the brain.

I'm not being sarcastic here, but can you tell me why you believe that evolution "designed" the heart with one coronary artery? Or perhaps you could tell me how you would have designed it? Two arteries? Three?

I have a few other questions. Which came first—the blood or the heart that pumps the blood? Did the body evolve a heart because it needed it? How did the body survive when the heart hadn't yet evolved? Or was the body alive without a heart? How did that work?

Did skin exist before the blood formed? How did the skin stay alive without blood? Why did blood form and how did skin live without oxygen pumping though it? If skin was able to live in that state, where did the oxygen come from, and why did the blood suddenly need oxygen to keep it alive? Did lungs form because they were needed to pull in oxygen for the heart? How long did it take for the lungs to evolve, and how did the heart survive without oxygen?

One more. Why have you been reading the posts of a "liar"? I think it would be wise to stop, because you and your atheist friends are just encouraging me. I like you being here, but you should understand that you are promoting Intelligent Design every time you write to me. That's not good for the dying cause of evolution or for atheism.

Why did God create marijuana? Seriously, educate me on this topic.

I have no idea *why* God created the marijuana plant. But it seems that everything He created has some purpose for some part of His creation. For example, hemp (from which marijuana is made) is very useful in creating strong rope.

Marijuana is often called "weed," and weeds came about on earth as a direct result of the curse of God, following Adam's sin.

If, however, you are *really* asking, "If God created marijuana, shouldn't we therefore smoke it?" I think I may be able to answer that. I would say that God also created sand. If you want to eat sand by the spoonful, go ahead. But don't complain when you get a bellyache.

While God had a practical use for marijuana, man decided for some reason to burn it and kill his brain cells by inhaling its harmful fumes. Likewise, man decided to use the beautiful poppy to destroy his life with incredibly addictive heroin.

Breathing in the burning fumes of *anything* isn't good for the human body. In fact, it's extremely unhealthy to do such a thing, and those who do so aren't thinking very deeply. Another word for marijuana is "dope." I wonder why?

Just how intelligent is a designer who puts nipples on a creature that will never suckle an infant?

I could say that male nipples are God's thumbtacks to keep the chest in place, but I'm sure one or two atheists would take me seriously. Still, it sounds better than the theory that they are the evolutionary beginnings of making men capable of nursing.

Talking of crazy imaginations, I just purchased a book called *The Wild World of the Future*.[13] It's a publication that imagines what animals will look like millions of years into the future. Professor Neil Alexander, the leading biologist who helped design many of the incredible creatures pictured in the book, encourages readers to make up their own creatures. He says, "Be bold when you imagine the animals of the future."[14] It's a good exercise. Evolution is all about imagination.

You too can play the game and do what the scientists have done. The sky is the limit. Take for instance, the common backyard snail. On page twenty-one you can see what they imagine it will look like in 200 million years' time. It will have evolved into a twelve-inch-high creature (about the size of a rabbit), and it will hop (like the rabbit). Its skin will be scaly as it will have evolved into a reptile. It could rightly be called a "snabbit." In just 100 million years, the slow-moving three-feet-high tortoise will have evolved into a massive creature forty times heavier than an elephant, and at twenty-three feet high, it will be the biggest creature on Earth. It will give up its hard shell, and have feet like an elephant. It could be called a "Tortephant." You can see a picture of it on page fifty. Also in 200 million years' time, one species of fish will have evolved wings and it will be able to truly fly. This isn't a stretch of the imagination because many evolutionists really believe that some dinosaurs developed feathers and became birds. Scientists have called the amazing flying fish a "flish." I didn't make up that name. It's in the book (page seventy-four). You can also meet the "bumblebeetle." No explanation needed for that one.

Obviously, this book was written for children, and it is billed as the "Companion book to the Discovery Channel series: *The Future is Wild*" (page ninety-six). For those adults who want to play "imagine," there's a book called *Future Evolution*, in which the author "foresees humankind's evolving alongside machines, in company with genetically altered plants that will infest the world as weeds and cloned animal species devoid of any evolutionary spark.

In April of 2007, during an ABC *Nightline* atheist debate, Kirk Cameron and I produced imaginary pictures of what we imagined would be genuine species-to-species transitional forms. We called one a "Crocoduck," and another was called a "birddog." This was to show exactly what evolutionists believe, but can't back up through the fossil record. We were ridiculed, called stupid, and told that we didn't understand evolution. However, these books vindicate us (not that we needed it). They have done with the future what evolutionists have done with the past. They have made a mockery out of science.

Chapter Two

OUR CONSCIENCE TESTIFIES TO A CREATOR AND OUR NEED FOR A SAVIOR

"In the science, evolution is a theory about changes;
in the Myth it is a fact about improvements.
To those brought up on the Myth, nothing seems more normal,
more natural, more plausible, than that chaos should turn into order,
death into life, ignorance into knowledge."

—C. S. LEWIS, "FUNERAL OF A GREAT MYTH"

A *group of self-appointed art experts* stood around a beautiful painting. They admired each brush stoke with its vibrant colors and sheer brilliance. The painting was utterly unique in style. It was a masterpiece.

One of the experts suddenly noticed a very small signature at the bottom of the painting. He leaned forward to take a closer look, stood back, and with utter disdain said the artist's name and used the "n" word to describe him. The experts hated this man and all of his work, simply because of his skin color. Immediately they took out a small knife and carefully scraped off the artist's name until it was no longer visible. They, in effect, tried to erase or deny the painter's very existence—just as some surrounded by this astounding creation every day try to deny its Creator.

God knows (and you know) why those who deny God's existence come up with the same arguments over and over. They, as the Bible says, "hate God without cause." They see the expression of His utterly brilliant handiwork. He gave them the gift of life itself, and painted the landscape of this world with breathtaking beauty, and they scrape any semblance of His name from the canvas. They disdain the God who gave them life. Why?

Creation points to the *existence* of a Creator, but its breathtaking beauty reveals the *nature* of that Creator. Our Creator didn't leave us sitting on a barren rock with only the barest of essentials we need for survival. In creation, we see the beautiful, the sublime, the amazing. We have herbs for food and medicine. We find peace in the soothing sound of a brook and laughter in the antics of a playful puppy. We sit in awe of majestic mountains and glistening stars. We have the ability to do more than hunt and gather food—the human mind has discovered and invented some incredible things. Creation, both in nature and in our own brains, offers so much more than what we need physically. It meets our emotional and spiritual needs as well.

The same Creator Who gave us all of this to enjoy clearly wanted true abundance for us—not mere survival. He loves us. An impersonal force like evolution, if real, would have left us sitting on that bare rock, because it wouldn't care about us beyond mere survival. But God does, and He proved it when He gave us this incredible planet to inhabit. The evidence of His existence and of His love is all around us. And, as mentioned in the last chapter, even atheists will have no excuse for denying Him on the Day of Judgment.

We humans have an implicit responsibility to the One Who gave us so much. We owe Him our worship, and obedience to His Law—*that* is why atheists hate Him so vehemently. Atheists want to be free from all moral or spiritual responsibilities, but their God-given conscience tells them deep down that they can't. That explains the intense reactions some of them display to the very name of God.

Atheists argue God doesn't exist. They argue if He does exist, the suffering in the world proves that He is vengeful or that He doesn't care. The suffering in the world is due to our living on a planet polluted by sin—not to God's hatred or neglect. Humans choose to murder when God gave us the intellect to cure disease. Humans choose to pollute when God gave us a pure planet rich in every resource we need. Each and every one of us will be held accountable one day. And we will have absolutely no excuse when standing before God. We obviously cannot keep God's Law on our own. Every attempt ever made in history at creating Utopia or living morally perfect lives has failed. We need a Savior, and atheists detest that fact.

And it's clear that, just as the experts aggressively removed the painter's name from the painting to try to blot out his existence, atheists have an aggressive agenda to remove God's name from schools, from currency, from nature programs and history books, and at the same time fill movies and television with His name used in blasphemy.

But our concern isn't for God. The Bible says, "God is not mocked. Whatever a man sows, that shall he reap" (Galatians 6:7). All atheists are doing is storing up wrath that will be revealed on the Day of Judgment. They act like a stunted, blind and crippled flea shaking his rebellious little fist at a massive herd of ten thousand wild stampeding elephants. They had better move out of the way while they still have time.

A common misconception is that polygraphs detect lies. They don't. They measure body responses. There is some correlation between these responses and lying; but there is also considerable room for error. Some people can "fail" a polygraph just because they are nervous about the situation in which they find themselves.

Our atheist friend is right. The "lie" detector isn't a lie detector; it actually is a "conscience" detector. It detects the body's physical reactions to the voice of the conscience. We did an entire program on this subject for the third season of our TV program, in which we hooked Kirk up to a polygraph machine and he tried to beat the machine. You won't believe what happened.

The conscience is a dilemma for the believer in evolution. He doesn't know why it exists. Neither do the experts. Why would evolution create something that tells us that it's wrong to lie, to steal, to kill, and to commit adultery? Was primitive man committing these sins before he evolved a conscience? If he wasn't, why did the conscience evolve? If he was, why did the conscience evolve?

Rather, the conscience is the inner light that God has given to every one of us, and He will hold us responsible to it. We will have no excuse on Judgment Day, because we know right from wrong. And that guilt manifests itself in sweaty palms, alterations in our breathing patterns, and our heart rhythm. So don't sweat it. Listen to its voice. It should bring you to the foot of a blood-stained Cross.

Isn't it more logical and reasonable to say that your conscience is put there by society—that your parents, neighbors, teachers, and authority figures (police, elected officials, preachers, and others) all play a role in forming your morality as you grow from infant to adult? This is a more sensible explanation, because it explains why different cultures have slightly different moralities.

It is interesting that every culture has a sense of morality, and that no matter how "primitive" they are, they acknowledge some sort of Creator. I am not aware of any past culture that has been found to be atheistic.

However, let's say that you are right—that it is society and not God that entirely shapes the human conscience. Let's imagine that a man has been rescued by authorities after twenty years of being raised by wolves. He is found to be intelligent and completely sane, but has had no moral instruction from any human being in those twenty years.

He is cleaned up, given a nice suit, and taken to New York, where he is overawed by what he sees. He is still given no moral instruction. When he is left alone, the first thing he does is find a pretty young woman. He rapes and murders her, then he steals her money and is captured while spending it.

In court, his attorney's defense is that he didn't know right from wrong—society had given him no moral instruction. Is the judge going to let him go? Of course not, because although the human conscience may be influenced by society, etc., it is not given to us by society. It is given to us by God, so that every sane human being intuitively knows right from wrong. That's why we will all be without excuse on the Day of Judgment.

There is a reason every culture acknowledges God. It's because the knowledge of His existence is manifest through the conscience, as well as through creation:

> [B]ecause what may be known of God is manifest in them, for God has shown it to them. For since the creation of the world His invisible attributes are clearly seen, being understood by the things that are made, even His eternal power and Godhead, so that they are without excuse, because, although they knew God, they did not glorify Him as God, nor were thankful, but became futile in their thoughts, and their foolish hearts were darkened (Romans 1:19-21).

I have a perfectly functional conscience. It nags me when I don't give time and money to charity, it demands that I tell the truth when telling a lie would be more convenient, it (for the most part) holds me back from saying cruel-yet-witty things even when I dearly want to...And yet, oddly enough, my conscience has absolutely nothing to say on the subject of my atheism. Now why is that? Is my conscience broken, or is your definition just bogus?

This is a very good question because it brings out a very good point. You acknowledge that your conscience addresses you in the area of morality. It accuses you of selfishness (failing to fulfill the Law that says you should love your neighbor as yourself—giving to charities, being kind, etc.). It accuses you when you lie—violating the Ninth Commandment. This is because God has written "the work of the Law" on your heart, so that your conscience will accuse you of transgression of that Law (see Romans 2:15).

However, the reason your conscience has nothing to say about your atheism is that atheism is not a moral issue. It's an intellectual issue. If I were to lie or steal, my conscience would scream at me. But if I said something that was intellectually stupid, like one and one make five, the conscience would remain silent. The same applies with the foolishness of atheism.

CAN HUMANS BE GOOD WITHOUT GOD?

I think that men who don't have God can be good, normal people, just not perfect.

It deeply concerns me when I hear a professing Christian tell an atheist that an atheist can be a good person. There is a reason for my concern. Jesus said that there is no one good but God (see Mark 10:18). Anyone who says that human beings are good is calling Jesus a liar. My concern isn't just that the atheist is being confirmed in his deception, but it makes me doubt the genuine nature of the Christian's salvation, because it seems that he has no biblical knowledge of sin himself. This deception comes when the Law is not used to bring the knowledge of sin (see Romans 3:19-20), and to show sin to be "exceedingly sinful" (see Romans 7:13).

Not surprisingly, he believes that preaching the Gospel simply means to tell people "Jesus loves you," something for which there is no precedent in Scripture. Wherever the love of Christ is preached, it's almost always in direct co-relation to the Cross (see John 3:16; Romans 5:8; etc.), and the Cross makes no sense without mentioning sin, and sin makes no sense without preaching the Law, for "sin is transgression of the Law" (see 1 John 3:4).

I thought I was a good person until I understood that in *God's* Book, "good" means to be morally perfect. The only just rule by which we can measure our morality is by the Ten Commandments. The Ten Commandments are like a mirror in which we can see our sin; we can see how deeply we fail God. It was through the moral Law that I found that God considers lust to be adultery and hatred to be murder. When I measured myself by *that* standard, I realized I am not good. At all.

It's also not surprising that the atheist has kind words for the Christian. This is because he is not offended by his message. However, to fail to warn sinners of the terrible consequences of sin (damnation in hell), and to instead tell them that they are good people, is the ultimate betrayal. Jesus warned, "Woe unto you, when all men shall speak well of you, for so did their fathers to the false prophets" (Luke 6:26).

One need not be a born again Christian to be a good person. In fact, there is an elderly couple who lives down the road from me. For several years now my son and I have shoveled their walks when it snows. My Christian neighbor said to me one day, "I saw you and your son shoveling down at Joe's yesterday. My wife and I pray for them often." I wanted to laugh in his face. I think you know why.

A Christian is not a "good person." The reason for this is that no one can be called a good person when we have no clear definition of the word *good*. Is a rapist a good person because he no longer rapes? Or does a thief become a good person when he gives to charity? Some would say "Yes," and others would say "No."

The only way to define who is good and who isn't is to define the word *good*. The dictionary has fifty-eight definitions for the word, but the principle meaning is to be "morally excellent." In other words, to be *good* means to be morally perfect in thought, word, and deed. The Bible tells us that only God is good (see Mark 10:17). Even the word is derived from the word *God*. So once there's a clear definition, it's clear that a Christian is not a good person. Neither is a non-Christian.

In the above objection, the person implies that you don't have to be a Christian to live a good life. That's true. Anyone can do the things that Christians do. They can start hospitals, schools, feed the poor, build houses, etc. But that won't get anyone to heaven, nor will it save anyone from hell. This is because salvation has nothing to do with our "good" works. How could it? What could you and I ever do to "earn" everlasting life?

But add to the equation the fact that we are criminals, having violated the Law of a holy God a multitude of times, and it becomes clear that the only way any of us could ever be saved from hell and enter heaven is by the mercy of the Judge. And that's what the Bible teaches. A Christian is saved by the grace and mercy of God, without works: "For by grace are you saved through faith; and that not of yourselves. It is the gift of God, not of works lest any man boast" (Ephesians 2:8-9).

So stop pretending to be good, and realize that doing good will do you no good on Judgment Day. Instead, repent and trust the

Savior, and then live a good life—not to impress anyone or bribe God, but out of gratitude to Him for His mercy.

Can't you at least acknowledge that people who are POLITE, HONEST, FORTHCOMING, HOSPITABLE, GENUINE, CONGENIAL, AMIABLE, and TRUSTWORTHY (and possibly, kind to old ladies, pets, and children) are "good people," simply meaning that they are (a) not a threat, (b) personable, reasonable, (c) friendly, (d) neighborly???

Great point. You are talking about "good" from a human point of view (the only point of view in which you believe). But, let's face it; if you find a human being that is always polite, honest, hospitable, genuine, congenial, amiable, and trustworthy, you haven't found someone who is good; you have found someone who is "remarkable." Perhaps this is why there are so many divorces. Many a man is kind, amiable, and trustworthy before the wedding day. The knight's shining armor gets a little dull and rusty in time.

However, there is something else that comes into the equation when God is involved, and it's a life and death issue. I have interviewed hundreds, if not thousands, of people on television and on radio, and I have found by experience that the Bible is right when it says that every man will almost always speak of his own goodness (you probably did it when I spoke of finding people who are always polite, honest, hospitable, amiable, etc.). They are sure that they are morally good, until they understand that God's standard of goodness (the one He will judge us with on Judgment Day), is infinitely higher than theirs.

Let's take Joe Average. He is polite, hospitable, genuine, congenial, amiable, and trustworthy. He is a remarkably good person—by human standards. However, when measured by God's standards, he proves to be a liar, a thief, a blasphemer, and an adulterer at heart. He has violated God's Law, and is therefore a lawbreaker. These sins we take so lightly are extremely serious charges in the sight of a morally perfect God. I can't express to you how serious lying and blasphemy and adultery are to God. Under His Law, they demand the death sentence.

Humility Test

Get ready. I'm going to boast, and your reaction will test if you are humble or proud. Chickens are about as dumb a creature as you can get. I know because we have some. We live in an area that is zoned for chickens (and humans). They are dumb (the chickens), but they do what we can't. They make fresh eggs for us each morning. How cool is that? Isn't God wonderful? (Monitor your reaction to that statement.) He made the chicken first, then they make the eggs…and they make them for us. We made them a cozy nest, and they make their way there each day and lay eggs for us to eat. God is amazing (monitor your reaction again). But more than that, the chickens let us know when they have finished laying (they let out a loud chicken noise—English translation "It's done!"), so that we can go out and collect the edible egg.

Did you know that if you hold a chicken in the palm of your hand (on its back), it goes really docile? It's almost hypnotized. Perhaps it does that so that if we want chicken for dinner, there won't be any resistance. That means we can have tender chicken breast, Kentucky fried chicken, hot wings, cold wings, chicken casserole…you name it, you can have it. God is so good, and so kind to us. Psalm 34:2 says "My soul shall make its boast in the Lord; the humble shall hear of it and be glad." Are you glad to hear God being given praise? Your reaction will reveal if you are humble of heart, or if you are possessed by the arrogance of pride.

So now everything changes for Joe Average the lawbreaker (criminal). Let's say a man is found in court. The charges are extremely serious—rape and murder. He says, "Judge, I am guilty of raping and killing that woman, but I want you to know that I am polite, hospitable, genuine, congenial, amiable, and trustworthy." Can you see that such a boast when he is guilty of heinous crimes is detestable?

If you don't trust in Jesus Christ, you are just like that criminal. You, like me, have violated God's Law a multitude of times, and your sins are very serious in God's sight. The fact that you may use your manners, or that you are amiable to people, isn't irrelevant to your case. The truth is that boasting of your own so-called morality is detestable in God's sight. Jesus said to those who did that, "You are those who justify yourselves before men, but God knows your hearts. For what is highly esteemed among men is an abomination in the sight of God" (Luke 16:15).

The only thing you and I can do to be saved from being thrown into God's prison (hell) is to trust in His mercy...and the Bible says that He is rich in mercy to all that call upon Him. Please call upon Him today.

I hope my ethics have the practical results of causing less harm to life and liberty, and dealing justice as humanely as possible, than any ethical teachings of any church.

The Christian's eternal salvation (the fact that he has eternal life) has nothing to do with him being "good," or having an ethical code. If a criminal is shown mercy by a good judge and his case is dismissed, it wasn't dismissed on the basis of the criminal's goodness or his standard of ethics. It was entirely on the basis of the goodness of the judge. And the sinner (a criminal in God's eyes) has his case dismissed (has his sins forgiven) because of God's goodness, not because of anything he has done.

Then, if the criminal has truly seen the kindness of the judge, he will leave his criminal life behind. This is done entirely out of appreciation for the judge's goodness in dismissing his case. And that is the Gospel in a nutshell. I was guilty of violating God's Law—which says that He sees lust as adultery, hatred as murder. His ethical standards are so high, lying lips are an "abomination" (extremely detestable) to Him. Yet, His amazing grace (mercy) dismissed the case of a wretch like me.

I now live an ethical life out of an appreciation for mercy. This ethical life may or may not be as ethical as that of an atheist, but that will have no bearing at all on Judgment Day. God will judge the world in perfect righteousness, and only those who have called upon His mercy will be saved from His terrible justice.

Lusting after women or property...who cares? That thought is a crime is absurd. If you don't act on it, why should you be punished? Even if you dwell on it.

The thought that merely thinking could be a crime does seem absurd. Absurd, that is, until you realize that if you are caught thinking about killing the president of the United States, you will find yourself in serious violation of civil law. You don't have to do the act. You simply have to be thinking about it.

So what would our skeptical questioner say to that? Let me try to predict his words. He would probably say something like, "That's different. Conspiracy to murder the president is a serious crime." And that's the point. He doesn't think that pornography of the mind is a serious crime. God does. Our questioner's moral standards are extremely low. God's are incredibly high. If you and I have a seething hatred in our heart for another person, God sees that as murder. And if we burn with unlawful sexual thoughts toward another human being, God sees that as adultery.

So, to answer our skeptic's question, "Lusting after women or property...who cares?" God cares. He cares about justice big time, and He will see to it that the guilty will get their just dessert. Adulterers and murderers will end up damned in a terrible place called hell. Who cares? I do, and I'm not the only one.

I have seen a couple mentions of Ray's "good person test." So, I think it appropriate for me to comment on it. The Jesus presented in the Bible fails this test (lied and dishonored his mother). The God of the Old Testament likewise fails the test. (According to Ray, a single instance of anger is an automatic failure). The biblical God has many.

Wow. It amazes me that anyone would dare point to Jesus Christ in moral judgment. You had better have clean hands and a pure heart before you point a finger at the Son of God. I can't think of an appropriate metaphor. It's like a flea shouting abuse at a massive elephant, as the flea stands under the shadow of the elephant's great foot. Nope. That doesn't cut it. It's like a heinous criminal, who is so morally corrupt he makes Hitler seem like a Boy Scout, yelling obscenities at a good judge. Nope. That doesn't cut it.

Jesus never sinned once, in thought, word, or in deed. He never lied, stole, hated, lusted, coveted, murdered, or dishonored his parents.

Let's now turn the mirror back to you. When was the last time you burned with unlawfully sexual fantasies? You don't need to reply to that. God knows the answer. He knows all about you and

41

your most secret of sins. So take a little advice from a fellow sinner—stop pointing your sin-stained finger at perfection, and instead look at your own self-righteous and duplicitous heart, before it's too late.

What a depressing belief system you subscribe to. Humankind is intrinsically evil? I don't buy it. Are we capable of evil? Sure. But we're also capable of good. For instance, while taking a walk one time, I saw a hummingbird on the road. I picked it up to get it out of danger, and I warmed it up (it was a cold day) in my hand. Eventually, it recovered from whatever shock it was in and it flew off. If I was intrinsically evil, then I would have smashed it, or I would have simply left it lying on the street. Your assertions make absolutely no sense.

The reason you think that you aren't intrinsically evil is because you have your own standard of "goodness." God's standard is absolute perfection in thought, word, and deed. It means to love the One who gave you life with all of your heart, mind, soul, and strength. Do you love God like that? It also means to love your neighbor as much as you love yourself. "Neighbor," according to the Bible, is all of humanity. Have you done that? I certainly haven't. Let's see if you have. Have you ever lied to or stolen something from your neighbor (any other person)? If you have, you are a lying thief, irrespective of the "color" of the lie or the value of the item you stole.

Human nature trivializes lying and theft. God, however, doesn't. Because they are so counter to His perfectly holy nature, they are extremely serious in His sight. Have you used His name in vain (blasphemy)? Jesus said, "Whoever looks at a woman to lust for her has already committed adultery with her in his heart." Have you ever done that? Let's presume that you have red blood in your veins, and that you, like the rest of us, have violated God's Law. So, now the scenario changes. Now you are not a good person with a few moral weaknesses. Rather, in God's sight, you are a desperately wicked criminal with a multitude of crimes against God Himself. (Try to estimate how many times you have committed adultery in your heart by lusting after a woman, or how many lies you have told throughout your lifetime.)

So how will you justify yourself on Judgment Day, when every secret sin comes out as evidence of your guilt, including your thought life and the deeds you have done in darkness? Your sins are heinous in the sight of a holy God. The Bible says that they stir His just wrath (see John 3:36). What will you say? What would you think of a man who said, "Judge, I raped and murdered that woman, but I picked up a sick bird and didn't kill it. You should therefore let me go"? In doing so, he somehow thinks he balances the scales of justice. He offers kindness to a sick bird as payment for raping and murdering a woman. What sort of twisted individual would he be to say that?

No, there's nothing we can do to justify ourselves. We can only throw ourselves on the mercy of the Judge…and God is rich in mercy to all who call upon Him. He made a way for your "case" to be dismissed. Two thousand years ago, a legal transaction took place between God and mankind. We broke God's Law (the Ten Commandments) and He became a person in Jesus of Nazareth and paid our penalty in His life's blood. Now, because of the suffering, death, and resurrection of the Son of God, our case can be dismissed. God can forgive our sins and commute our death sentence. "God demonstrates His own love toward us, in that while we were still sinners, Christ died for us" (Romans 5:8). What you and I have to do in response to that is repent (turn from all sin) and trust in the Savior.

In English bowls, there is something called the "bias." This makes the ball curve one way when it is bowled. Until we are regenerated by the Holy Spirit, we will have a bias toward sin. However, the moment we repent and trust the Savior, we receive a new heart that *wants* to please God. How incredible!

What if someone says they don't believe we'll be judged by the Law?

The Bible makes it clear that there will be a Day of Judgment. The Scriptures warn, "Though hand join in hand [though the whole world says otherwise] the wicked shall not be unpunished…" (Proverbs 11:21). However, there are those who question the standard of judgment—will it be the Ten Commandments—the moral Law? Some say that it will rather be the words of Jesus that

43

will judge mankind. This belief is based on John 12:48: "He that rejects me, and receives not my words, has one that judges him: the word that I have spoken, the same shall judge him in the last day."

Humanity will be judged by the words of Jesus, but remember that the Scriptures say that God would "magnify the law and make it honorable" (Isaiah 42:21). This was the essence of the teaching ministry of the Messiah. The religious leaders had twisted the Law and demeaned it so that its original intent was lost. But Jesus magnified it. He showed them that lust was adultery, and that anger without cause violated its holy precepts, etc. He reminded them that not one jot or tittle of the Law would fail.

When Paul preached on Mars Hill he warned the idolatrous Athenians that God would judge the world "in righteousness." They had violated the first and second of the Ten Commandments and he therefore warned them that God was not "graven by art and man's device." The "righteousness" of which he spoke is the righteousness which is of the Law: "For as many as have sinned without law shall also perish without law: and as many as have sinned in the law shall be judged by the law" (Romans 2:12). James 2:12 also warns that the moral Law will be the standard of judgment: "So speak, and so do, as they that shall be judged by the law of liberty."

Those who may be tempted to say that the "law of liberty" isn't the moral Law but "the law of Christ" should look at the context. The preceding verse says: "For he that said, Do not commit adultery [Seventh Commandment], said also, Do not kill [Eighth Commandment]. Now if you commit no adultery, yet if you kill, you have become a transgressor of the law" (James 2:11).

If you use the Law to reach the lost, you may have had some people say that "taking God's name in vain" is not considered "blasphemy." However, the Greek word used is *blasphemia*. It breaks down to *blas* which means "against God or sacred persons or things," and *phemia* which means "speech." The Apostle Paul considered himself a blasphemer before his conversion (1 Timothy 1:13). He more than spoke against Jesus of Nazareth; he so hated Christianity, he killed Christians. So if any speech against God, and using His name without due respect is considered blasphemy, how much more evil is it to use His name as a cuss word?

Another accusation often leveled at us is that the Seventh Commandment is about "adultery," not fornication (sex before marriage). That's not true. 1 Timothy 1:8-10 makes clear that the Commandment not only includes fornicators, but it also includes homosexuals.

Finally, there are some who say that the Ninth Commandment says, "Thou shalt not bear false witness." They maintain that that is solely a reference to giving false witness in a court of law, and therefore doesn't include everyday lying. Another untruth. 1 Timothy 1:8-10 also says that the Law was made for liars. So, as much as the world would like to do away with the Law, or at least water it down, it's immutable. It's not going away, and it will be the unbending standard of judgment on the day when God judges the hearts of men and women (see Romans 2:12).

Had any of you been born in Saudi Arabia, Iraq, Iran, Jordan, Syria, etc., there is nearly a 100 percent chance that you would be Muslim, and no amount of free will given to you from Jesus would prevent that.

The Law of God is the key to understanding the dealings of God with humanity. The moral Law (the Ten Commandments) shows us that God is morally perfect, and because of His love of justice, He must by nature punish wrongdoing. If a man murders, justice must be done. If a man rapes, steals, commits adultery, lies, covets, etc., God's justice hovers over him. Once the Law comes into the equation it shows us that He owes humanity nothing but justice. He has no obligation to bless us with health or save us from death. All that comes by His mercy, something that doesn't come because we deserve it, but because God is merciful.

So if God sees fit to save someone in America, He does so because of His goodness. If He saves someone in Iraq, India, China, or Japan, He does so because He is good, and He reveals His goodness by sending missionaries to those countries so that they will hear the Gospel. Some countries forbid Christian missionaries from proclaiming the message of everlasting life. Other countries permit it.

The Bible says that no one comes to the Son unless the Father draws Him, and God draws whom He will to Himself whether the person to whom He is extending mercy lives in Iraq, New Zealand, China, Japan, or the United States.

But don't use that fact as an excuse to stay in your sins. Scripture tells us that He commands every one of us to repent (see Acts 17:30-31), because He has appointed a day in which He will judge the world in righteousness. That's not an option.

Why did God give us sexual desire if it's a bad thing? Even if you only lust over your spouse, you would most likely have felt lust for them before you married. After all, lust plays a big part in our choice of marriage partner. So why did God set us up to fail?

You seem to be confusing lust and sexual desire. God did give us sexual desire and it's not a bad thing. In fact, it's a good thing. How else would we be attracted to a prospective spouse, and why would we even procreate if there was no "desire"?

So, what then is the difference between sexual attraction and lust? One dictionary says that "lust" is "uncontrolled or illicit sexual desire or appetite; lecherousness." Or to put it another way, lust is pornography of the mind.

How then do we know the difference between "looking" and lusting? The answer is to listen to your God-given conscience. It will tell you...if you have a mind to listen. There's nothing wrong with simply seeing someone and having the automatic thought that she's attractive. But that's different from then formulating sexual thoughts about that person to lust for her. In case you're having trouble hearing from your conscience, here's another clue to help you: How would you feel if your spouse were doing that behavior? Would you mind it if she was entertaining lustful thoughts for other men, having sexual fantasies about someone other than you? We often have a hard time seeing wrong behavior in ourselves, but have no trouble seeing it in others.

So God isn't the one to blame for "setting us up to fail." To believe that would be like a criminal saying to a judge, "Judge, I raped that woman, but it really isn't my fault. God made me with sexual desire so it's His fault." If that won't hold water in a court of law, it's not going to be a valid defense on Judgment Day.

Look at how serious lust is in God's sight:

> You have heard that it was said to those of old, "You shall not commit adultery." But I say to you that whoever looks at a woman to lust for her has already committed adultery with her in his heart. If your right eye causes you to sin, pluck it out and cast it from you; for it is more profitable for you that one of your members perish, than for your whole body to be cast into hell. And if your right hand causes you to sin, cut it off and cast it from you; for it is more profitable for you that one of your members perish, than for your whole body to be cast into hell (Matthew 5:27-30).

However, our real problem isn't lust. That's just one large branch of the tree of our sinful nature. If we want to avoid the damnation of hell, we have to (with the help of God) take an axe to the root of the tree, and that can be done only through repentance toward God and faith in Jesus Christ.

You may have skipped over the words "damnation of hell," but that is a good motivating factor to repent. Let me put it another way. If I said to you that you need to give up chocolate, you would probably be horrified. However, if I proved to you that if you ate any more chocolate, it would kill you, you would then have a strong motivation to give it up, despite it being so palatable to your taste. So give the issue some serious thought. It's your choice...and it's your eternity.

Chapter Three

HUMANITY'S SIN
DESERVES PUNISHMENT

"Physical death is the first down payment for the wages of sin.
After death, there is hell to pay."

L et me tell you about my father. He regularly left my mom to take care of us kids (when he was around, there were times that he physically beat us). I remember him once killing a defenseless animal with his bare hands. With that information, you would be quite justified in saying that my father was a tyrant—an abusive pig of a man.

Here's some missing information. He regularly left Mom to take care of us because he was a builder and he worked long hours to make money to buy food for his beloved family. He did physically spank us when we lied or stole anything. He cared enough to correct us when we did wrong. Oh, and that helpless animal? He found it on the side of the road. It had been hit by a car and was dying. He put the poor animal out of its misery, and it grieved him to have to do it. My dad was a loving father and an extremely compassionate person.

Quote mine the Bible and you can, as some atheists do, paint God as a tyrant. But let me give you some more information. God gave us life. He gave us eyes to see the incredible creation He made for us. He gave us ears to hear the wonderful music He created for us. He gave us taste buds to enjoy all the incredible variety of food He made for us. And we use His name as a cuss word. We are unthankful and ungrateful for the unspeakable goodness He lavished upon us. So what did He do? He became a perfect Man in the person of Jesus of Nazareth. The first time Jesus opened His mouth to preach, they tried to kill Him. Scripture records that humanity tried to murder Him ten times before He reached the Cross. But that's why He came. This incredibly kind, loving, and forgiving God is also a God of justice and truth. His very nature demands that when a man murders another human being he must be punished. His justice demands that when a man rapes a woman, he must be punished for his crime. His righteousness cries out for justice to be done when anyone transgresses His perfect Law. So what did God do? He gave His life on an unspeakably cruel cross, taking the punishment for the sin of the world, so that evil humanity could escape being justly punished in hell.

So when I see Bible quote mining, I have a balance. I don't see my Father as a tyrant because Scripture gives me extra information that tells me that He is just and holy, and that all His judgments are righteous and true altogether. That terrible Cross shows me that His wrath hasn't changed, but it also shows me unspeakable love and mercy, goodness and kindness, compassion and care.

If I have a question about the character of God, I have the good sense to hold my hand upon my mouth until I am in heaven, and there God may see fit to answer it.

Mockers think that they have a "smoking gun" as evidence against God, and are the sort of people in the front row of a lynching mob. In truth, they are building their own gallows. They can't see clearly because they have a sequoia in their eye.

If the skeptic still wants to complain that God killed women and children in the Old Testament, he should realize that He did more than that. He proclaimed the death sentence on the *entire* human race—every man, woman, and child. We will all die because we have sinned against God. So if you are a skeptic, stop whining, get right with Him through the Savior, and escape the damnation of hell, while you still have time.

I know that we are to fear God because of His just punishment, but can you please tell me the reference to where the Bible says God is actually our enemy? Jesus actually said to his disciples that he was their friend.

Colossians 1:20-22 says, "And, having made peace through the blood of His Cross, by Him to reconcile all things unto Himself; by Him, I say, whether they be things in earth, or things in heaven. And you, that were sometime alienated *and enemies in your mind by wicked works,* yet now hath He reconciled in the body of His flesh through death, to present you holy and unblameable and unreproveable in His sight..." (italics added). The carnal *mind* is at enmity (in a state of hostility) against God (see Romans 8:7). The unregenerate mind spits out blasphemy, unbelief, and rebellion at God and His moral Law.

Jesus said, "You are my friends, *if you do whatsoever I command you*" (John 15:14, italics added). You forgot the second part of the verse. We are enemies of God as long as we are friends with this sinful world (see James 4:4-5).

If your only reason for believing in God is the fear of punishment, that's not a benevolent relationship. That's fear mongering, and I'm surprised you endorse it, Ray.

I "believed" in God for twenty-two years as a non-Christian, and "fear" had nothing to do with it. Let me give you a little background. My mom (who is still alive) is Jewish, and my father was a Gentile. My dad died a few years ago, but it was nothing serious. He was a Christian. For many years he "believed" in God, but there was no evidence that he knew the Lord until two weeks before he died. It took a heart attack to bring him to his senses.

I was born for the first time a few years after the Second World War, so rather than put "Jewish" on my birth certificate, my parents put "Methodist" in case there was another holocaust. Then they left me without any instruction about God. My point is that even without a moment of instruction from my parents, I fully "believed" in God. The reason I believed in a Creator was simply because I had a brain. Even as a child I knew that if there was a creation, logic told me there was a Creator. The dictionary can help those who are a little slow to figure this out by checking the words "creation" and "Creator":

Creation—noun, "the Creation, the original bringing into existence of the universe by God." *Creator*—noun, "the Creator, God."

While "fear mongering" is bad, never discount "fear" itself as being bad. Fear stops you from stepping off a five hundred-foot cliff. It keeps you away from fire. It holds you back from sticking a fork into a live power outlet. These types of fear are self-preserving, but the ultimate self-preserving fear is the fear of the Lord. That fear is called "the beginning of wisdom," and because of it, the Bible says men "depart from sin."

The reason anyone should fear God is because He is to be feared. Those who don't fear God haven't begun to be wise. Jesus gave these sobering words about the terror of falling into the hands of the Living God. He said, "And I say to you, My friends, do not be afraid of those who kill the body, and after that have no more that they can do. But I will show you whom you should fear: Fear Him who, after He has killed, has power to cast into hell; yes, I say to you, fear Him!" (Luke 12:4-5). On Judgment Day, those who think such talk is "fear mongering" will find out that it's not. It is simply the truth, and they will wish to God (understatement) that they had obeyed the Gospel.

DEATH AND HELL

"How much less man, who is a maggot! And a son of man, who is a worm!" (Job 25:6, Amplified Bible). Why would the Bible compare us to a lowly worm?

Perhaps it's because we are helpless. A lowly crawling worm epitomizes blind helplessness. If you see a worm making its way across your driveway and you want to stomp on it, it has no resistance. It has no legs, so it can't run. It has no arms or hands or claws to fend you off. It doesn't have a hiss, a growl, or a bite to scare you. It just lies there awaiting the fate of your big, fat foot. *Squish*, and it's gone.

That's how you are when it comes to death. It hovers over you like a big, fat foot. You lie under its terrible shadow. It's that close.

The Bible says that you live in "the shadow of death," and there's nothing you can do about it.

However, when Jesus was born, we are told, to them that "sat in the shadow of death, a light...sprung up." The Light of the World (Jesus Christ) abolished death through His suffering on the Cross, and through His resurrection.

So if you call upon Him in repentance and faith today, He will rescue you from your greatest enemy. I'm not kidding you. He did it for me—blind, little, helpless, sinful Ray Comfort.

Everything living dies, everything dead rots, and everything rotten may serve as fertilizer for new life. It's the carbon cycle and I didn't make it up and I have better sense than to fight or even resent a naturally occurring process.

Skeptics often unwittingly talk in the language of "absolutes." They say that "no one" can know if God exists, or "no one" can know if there is life after death, or, as in this case, that "everything" dies and rots. Yet, those who talk in absolutes (as though they had absolute knowledge) reveal a *lack* of knowledge.

For a skeptic to say "no one knows what happens after death," he must know what *everyone* knows in order for him to *know* that no one knows. If he says that nobody knows, he must have access to every thought of every human being from the beginning of the human race until this very present second, because if anyone *does* know what happens after death, then he's dead wrong. So, to be truthful, he is forced to say, "With the limited knowledge I have at present, I have come to the conclusion that no one knows what happens." So he really doesn't know at all.

The professing atheist is in the same small boat. He can't say, "There is no God" and be truthful. To do so he has to have access to all knowledge. So he has to say, "With the limited knowledge I have at present, I have come to the conclusion that there is no God. But I really don't know." So, in truth, every professing atheist is an "agnostic." He doesn't *know* and therefore can never be certain that God, heaven, and (more importantly) hell don't exist.

Again, the person who maintains that *everything* dies believes that he has access to *all* knowledge about *everything* living. Big words, but small thoughts. The skeptic isn't aware that God *never* dies. What's more, God promises that any living human being who comes to Him through repentance and faith in Jesus will not perish, but have everlasting life.

Don't believe it? That's your problem. You believe what secular science says, so just expand your beliefs. Take one small step of faith. Soften your hard heart. That one small step of faith will be the first step toward knowing and trusting the God who is life, gave you life, and offers you eternal life.

I'll be okay because when I die I will have paid for my sins, since the Bible says "the wages of sin is death." I'm going to live life to the fullest now, because when I die that's the end.

It's obvious that those who say such things believe the Bible because they have not only quoted it, but they are gambling the whole of their eternity on the meaning of one word—"death." They make the assumption that it simply means the "termination" of existence. But it doesn't, and a little reasoning should reveal that fact. Take Hitler for instance. He was responsible for the cruel deaths of six million Jews, many of whom were children. Was his death the "wages" of his unspeakably terrible sins? If death is the end, then God has given you the exact same wages as Hitler. That would mean that God is unjust, which is unthinkable.

The person who believes that our demise is the end is in for the shock of his death. There is going to be a resurrection of what the Bible calls, "the just and the unjust." This is not a resurrection of those who are good and those who are bad. The Scriptures tells us that there are no "good" people. Not one (see Psalm 14:1-4; Mark 10:18). There are only those who have been made "just" before God by the shed blood of Jesus Christ.

When we are found out to have done something wrong, we will often try to "justify" ourselves. We try to establish our innocence. In Christ, God freely justifies all those who come by childlike faith to the Savior. That means He proclaims us innocent—as though we had never sinned in the first place. However, those who die in their sins "fall into the hands of the Living God." That's a very fearful thing, because He will give them justice—their wages, and if that happens, there will be hell to pay.

I sincerely believe that if it were not for the great fear associated with the concept of hell that Christianity would never, ever have become the massive movement that it has throughout the ages. I also know, from firsthand experience, that the psychological damage that is done to children in the name of that fear is a horrid thing.

I think that you are right. The existence of hell is a legitimate reason to come to the Savior, and it is perhaps why so many profess faith in Christ. And your concerns about psychological damage may also be legitimate. I'm sure that many, in the name of Christianity, have hung its threat over the masses to keep them and their children in line. However, the biblical threat of hell is real and fearful, but God's offer of heaven is just as real and unspeakably wonderful. The threat without the offer is a horrid thing.

I can't speak to your firsthand experience, but I can say that none of my children, my grandchildren, or any of my friends' children have been psychologically damaged by the fear of hell. In fact, it's just the opposite. They don't fear hell at all, because they know that they have escaped it through faith in Jesus Christ.

I know, however, that many children have been psychologically damaged because of the fear of *death*. That's another legitimate fear. Death is a reality that all of us have to face. As an atheist, what do you tell your beloved children when they, with fear in their eyes, say, "Daddy, I don't want to die!"? Do you tell them that its nature's way, and that they just have to deal with it? Or do you tell them that they shouldn't think of negative things and to concentrate on life?

Christians don't need to cop out when that question is asked. We can tell our children how we were created (*you* don't know), why we were created (*you* don't know), why we are all going to die (*you* don't know), what happens after death (*you* don't know), and what we can do about it (*you* refuse to listen to that one).

Our society is filled with adults with psychological problems because they fear death. It terrorizes them every minute of every day. Millions live in quiet futility as they wait to die, and are driven to drugs, to the psychiatrist's couch, to alcohol, and to suicide, solely because of the fear of death.

The tragedy is that that fear could instantly leave them if they repented and placed their faith in the One who came to "deliver them who through fear of death were all their lifetime subject to bondage" (Hebrews 2:15).

The difference between the Bible and an instruction book is the myriad of untestable (and detestable) claims the Bible makes. How do you know that if I "sin" I will go to hell? Only from the Bible, which is a source of such dubious credibility as to be laughable. Can you prove to me that ANY of what the Bible claims about hell and "sin" is true? Can you prove to me that hell exists? If not, you, along with all your pulpit-pounding ilk, are nothing more than a carnival ride of empty threats.

Hell is no empty threat. If I believed it was, I wouldn't bother warning you. However, the way for you to avoid the subject is to say that you don't believe in God. That cuts the problem off for you at the Source. All you have to do is ignore your God-given common sense. He doesn't exist because you don't believe in Him. You could carry this further if you didn't like gravity, history, the wind, or love. Those things can't be seen, and therefore wouldn't exist if you didn't believe in them either. Anything that you don't like will not exist if you just say that you don't believe in it.

The key to being a committed atheist is to be totally unreasonable. When someone denies the obvious, you can't reason with them. That's why you can be presented with the absolute and clear evidence of creation (which screams of a Creator to any reasonable person), and you can say that there's no evidence for God.

If you were reasonable, I would say that we know that hell exists because we know intuitively that God is good. And if He is good, He must by nature punish a man who has tied up and raped three teenage girls, and then one by one, strangled them to death. In this case, justice delayed is not justice denied. God will bring that murderer to judgment and see that he gets exactly what he deserves, and hell is the place of God's justice. It's His prison. Common sense says that if God is good, it is right that He is also just. However, God is so good He will also punish thieves, liars, fornicators, adulterers, blasphemers, and everyone who has violated His perfect and holy Law. That leaves us all in big trouble. Without a Savior we will get exactly what we deserve, and that is a terrifying thing, whether we believe it or not. If you want proof, then simply repent and trust Jesus Christ, and you will know that what I am saying is the Gospel truth.

I just wanted to let you know that you're an @$#!! You start out talking to people by questioning them on their bad behaviors, then you tell them they're gonna burn in hell. After scaring them with this method you turn around and start running your mouth about Jesus and how he died for them and how you don't want to see them go to hell, which then makes them sad. You think you're getting results when you do this? You think you're changing lives? Maybe for those couple of seconds when you twist people's emotions around and warp their mind into believing they're terrible people and they will die and go to hell. You talk to them like you're the @!#$&! higher power! And you have the nerve to talk about self righteousness? You're a joke, take a good look in the mirror before you go out judging others. Who knows, that may be you burning in hell's eternal flames, and your little %$@!# buddy too...

This person is pretty upset and I can understand why. What right have I got to question people about their "bad behavior"? Why do I tell them about hell, and who God says will go there? If he thinks that I am standing in judgment over people I can see why he's mad. He's also right about each of us needing to look into the mirror. So let's deal with each of these questions.

It's true that I do ask people about their bad behavior, and I do tell them what the Bible says about hell. But how could I not? If I am fully persuaded that someone is in terrible danger, I have to at least warn them.

The mirror issue. I am as bad, if not worse than most of the people to whom I speak. I have broken all of the Ten Commandments, in spirit if not in letter. I have committed a multitude of sins, and that's why I need a Savior. Being a Christian means that all that sin is forgiven.

Now for the big one. The "judging" issue. I never judge anyone I interview. How could I? I don't know most of them. I don't know their thought life or what they do in darkness, so how could I judge them? All I know is what they have freely admitted. If someone says that he's a liar and a thief, I believe him. Then I tell him what the Bible says about sin and the fate of those who violate His Law. My motivation is one of love and concern. No other reason.

There is one thought that skeptics don't seem to take into account. *What if hell does exist? What if the Bible is right? What if God is holy and just and will punish murderers and rapists in a terrible place called hell? What if every single person will get what's coming to them?* If what we say is the gospel truth, then what we are saying is justified and most necessary.

Do I think that we are "getting results"? God knows. I plant the seed. He makes it grow.

So tell me, Ray, how do you feel about Jews? I don't believe they're hell bound; do you?

I am often asked that question when I am open air preaching. It usually comes from those who don't know their history. The disciples were Jewish. All of them. Jesus was Jewish (see John 4:9). We even have His genealogy to prove it (see Matthew 1:1-17). He was the promised Jewish Messiah (see Romans 15:12). Christianity was birthed in the land of the Jews, and not the United States as is commonly believed. The first three thousand converts to Christianity were Jews (see Acts 2:41), and the next five thousand to be converted were Jews. The Apostle Paul was Jewish (see Acts 23:6). The God of the Jews (the God of Israel) made sure the Gospel was offered to the Jews first, before the Gentiles (see Romans 1:16). I am Jewish because my mother is Jewish, and I'm a Christian. The usual response to that is to say that I can't be a Christian and a Jew at the same time. However, the last time I checked, I still had the same Jewish blood I was born with.

The advantage to the Jew when it comes to Christianity is that they have the moral Law to show them that they need a Savior (see Romans 3:1-2). However, eternal life is offered to all humanity, whether Jew or Gentile, black or white ("red and yellow, black and white, all are precious in His sight..."), or male or female. If anyone ends up in hell it will not be because of their ethnicity or their color. It will be because of their sin. Rapists, murderers, thieves, liars, blasphemers, adulterers, fornicators, etc., will get exactly what they deserve, and if I die in my sins, being Jewish will not save me from the justice of a holy God. Only the blood of Jesus of Nazareth, the God-given Jewish Messiah, can do that. And that same precious blood was shed for you, whether you are Jew or Gentile. Whosoever will may come.

THE FUTURE

Just how long are the "last days" supposed to last?... The Bible says that no one knows when the end will come, but then it gives some clues. And the clues it gives are all things that have happened since the dawn of human beans.

Yes, the questioner did write "beans" instead of "beings," revealing that he has a strange belief about where we sprouted from, or he's a big Mr. Bean fan, or he's just like the rest of us and makes mistakes when typing.

Human beings are prone to err, and the greatest error any of us can ever make is to be wrong about God. The religious leaders at the time of Christ made that mistake continually. They came to Jesus with questions for which they didn't really want answers. Instead, their intent was to trick Him so that they could catch Him in His words. One such time was when they asked Him about the resurrection. They concocted a scenario in which a woman had seven husbands who died one after the other. Then they asked, "In the resurrection, when they rise, whose wife will she be? For all seven had her as wife." Jesus answered, "Are you not therefore mistaken, because you do not know the Scriptures nor the power of God?" (See Mark 12:18-27 for the whole story.)

The same answer could be given to 90 percent of the questions asked by skeptics. According to the Bible, "The fear of the Lord is the beginning of wisdom; a good understanding have all those who do

His commandments" (Psalm 111:10). So a professing atheist who has no fear of God also has no understanding at all of the character and power of God. Even those of us who know Him know only a tiny drop in an infinite ocean of His greatness. He is omnipresent—He dwells everywhere, filling the infinitude of space. Every tiny atom in the universe is displayed before Him. He is omnipotent—nothing is impossible for God. He is omniscient—seeing every thought of every human heart. These thoughts are too much for human brains that can barely juggle a few thoughts at a time, let alone comprehend the greatness of the God who gave us life.

Skeptics also don't know the Scriptures. Most of the verses cited in questions are read with an ignorance of corresponding verses to give them their biblical context.

So, in answer to the question: God's timeframe is different from ours—"For a thousand years in Your sight are like yesterday when it is past..." (Psalm 90:4), and "...with the Lord one day is as a thousand years, and a thousand years as one day" (2 Peter 3:8). The Bible tells us that the "last days" began on the Day of Pentecost (see Acts 2:17). We have been in the last days for two thousand years (not much in God's timeframe). Most of the signs that the Bible speaks of have been around for many years; however, prophecies about the increase of travel and the increase of knowledge are far more evident in recent years. And, of course, the Jews obtaining Jerusalem in 1967 is the fulfillment that started the prophetic clock ticking. How long will the last days last? God only knows...but we are certainly getting close to when the door of His mercy closes.

This question raises (for me at least) the whole issue of the rapture. Proof for the existence of God? I think that would pretty much do it for me... According to the myth, people will vanish, the dead will rise and head off to heaven—and we will most likely be under the control of a Jewish, homosexual world leader... Let us not forget that we will also get a red moon and a black sun—a huge meteor will burn one third of grass and trees—200 million horse-like creatures will run rampant—oh, and fresh water will become blood. Tell you what, if all that bunk comes to pass—I will have another think about this god thing, I can't promise anything, even then, but I will certainly have another think. Really, water turned to blood and horse-like creatures—golly.

May I say respectfully, you may have been watching too many Hollywood movies, or the Discovery Channel, or maybe reading stuff on weird Web sites, or eating too much cheese before you go to bed (that can cause bad dreams).

I would suggest that you take a deep breath, then read the Bible with a humble heart, praying that God would show you what is prophetically symbolic and what is literal. If you don't do that, you will end up with the nightmare that you have just related. The Bible is a book filled with symbolism—from Ezekiel's wheels, to the dreams of Joseph and Daniel, to the Book of Revelation, and of course, many of the words of Jesus. Again, some things are literal, and some are symbolic.

When Jesus said that He was "the Door," He didn't mean a door with literal hinges that swing back and forth. He is the entry to heaven (see also John 14:6). When He said that His flesh was meat and we were to eat it, He wasn't speaking of cannibalism. We spiritually "taste and see that the Lord is good." When He held the cup of wine and said "This is My blood" and told us to drink it, He wasn't speaking of His literal blood (He couldn't have been, because His blood was still running through His veins).

Wine is often used as a symbol of blood—Jesus turned the water into wine at the Cana wedding, and God turned water into blood with the plagues of Egypt. All these symbols and events have hidden and wonderful meanings behind them for those who are willing to dig a little. If you think about it, things that we value in life usually have to be searched out—gold doesn't lie on top of the ground. You have to search for it. It's the same with silver, diamonds, pearls, etc., and it's the same with Biblical gems. You have to dig a little to find the riches.

As much as I would like to be, I am not a prophecy expert or even a prophecy buff. I don't get too deeply into it, because so many people end up with weird and strange scenarios, and what's more they all think that they have it right. I prefer to put my time into trying to reach people like you with the Gospel. Your salvation is infinitely more important to me than my eschatological interpretation.

"When they persecute you in one town, flee to the next; for truly I tell you, you will not have gone through all the towns of Israel before the Son of Man comes" (Matthew 10:23). "Truly I tell you, there are some standing here who will not taste death until they see that the kingdom of God has come with power" (Mark 9:1). All failed prophecies.

The key is the word "power" (in the verse you quoted—Mark 9:1). The Kingdom of God came with "power" on the Day of Pentecost (see Acts 1:8). Remember, there is a spiritual kingdom (see John 3:3), and a literal Kingdom (the one that will be set up on earth by God Himself). You are greatly mistaken when you say that they are failed prophecies. You neither know the Scriptures, nor the power of God.

You might say the Bible predicts events before they happen, but the problem is that the predictions claimed to be correct are not pointed out until after they happen. The Bible's predictions are vague enough that people aren't pointing out what and when it will happen; they take an event that has happened and adjust their interpretation to fit the event and claim the event is what the prediction said all along. God's predictions are not alone, it is done with Nostradamus, horoscopes, and tarot cards predictions, too.

I once believed that Nostradamus was able to somewhat predict the future. However, after closely studying him and his so-called predictions, I found that he stole his "prophecies" from the Bible (which he read in secret), revised them, and claimed them as his own. I even produced an award-winning documentary about this, and also wrote a book called *Nostradamus, Attack on America*.

He was able to plagiarize the prophecies of the Bible and get away with it because in those days the Roman Catholic Church forbade the reading of the Scriptures. Nowadays, as in his day, anyone who is ignorant of the Bible's prophecies will be impressed with the writings of Nostradamus. His "predictions," though, are incredibly generic (just as horoscopes and tarot cards are), and people can read into them any meaning they want to.

That isn't true with biblical prophecies. They are extremely detailed and precise. Unlike other books, the Bible offers a multitude of specific predictions—some thousands of years in advance—that either have been literally fulfilled or point to a definite future time when they will come true. No other religion has specific, repeated, and unfailing fulfillment of predictions many years in advance of events over which the predictor had no control. The sacred writings of Buddhism, Islam, Confucius, etc., are all missing the element of proven prophecy. These kinds of predictions are unique to the Bible.

Only one who is omniscient can accurately predict details of events thousands of years in the future. Limited human beings know the future only if it is told to them by an omniscient Being. God provided this evidence for us so we would know that the Scriptures have a divine Author: "For I am God, and there is no other; I am God, and there is none like Me, declaring the end from the beginning, and from ancient times things that are not yet done" (Isaiah 46:9-10).

In addition, the Bible declares that prophets must be 100 percent accurate—no exceptions. If anyone claimed to be speaking for God and the prophesied event didn't come to pass, he was proven to be a liar. The writings of Mormons and Jehovah's Witnesses are littered with false prophecies, so we can know whether they are written by men or by God.

The Bible's sixty-six books, written between 1400 BC and AD 90, contain approximately 3,856 verses concerned with prophecy. For example, the Scriptures predicted the rise and fall of great empires like Greece and Rome (Daniel 2:39-40), and foretold the destruction of cities like Tyre and Sidon (Isaiah 23). Tyre's demise is recorded by ancient historians, who tell how Alexander the Great lay siege to the city for seven months. King Nebuchadnezzar of Babylon had failed in a thirteen-year attempt to capture the seacoast city and completely destroy its inhabitants. During the siege of 573 BC, much of the population of Tyre moved to its new island home half a mile from the land city. Here it remained surrounded by walls as high as 150 feet until judgment fell in 332 BC with the arrival of Alexander the Great. In the seven-month siege, he fulfilled the remainder of the prophecies (Zechariah 9:4; Ezekiel 26:12) concerning the city at sea by completely destroying Tyre, killing eight thousand of its inhabitants and selling thirty thousand of its population into slavery. To reach the island, he scraped up the dust and rubble of the old land city of Tyre, just like the Bible predicted, and cast them into the sea, building a two-hundred-foot-wide causeway out to the island.

Alexander's death and the murders of his two sons were also foretold in the Scripture. Another startling prophecy was Jesus' detailed prediction of Jerusalem's destruction, and the further dispersion of Jews throughout the world, which is recorded in Luke 21. In AD 70, not only was Jerusalem destroyed by Titus, the future emperor of Rome, but another prediction of Jesus' in Matthew 24:1-2 came to pass—the complete destruction of the Temple of God.

Even more important are the many prophecies of a coming Messiah. God said He would send someone to redeem mankind from sin, and He wanted there to be no mistake about who that person would be. For example, in the Book of Daniel, the Bible prophesied the coming of the one and only Jewish Messiah prior to the Temple's demise. The Old Testament prophets declared He would be born in Bethlehem (Micah 5:2) to a virgin (Isaiah 7:14), be betrayed for thirty pieces of silver (Zechariah 11:12-13), die by crucifixion (Psalm 22), and be buried in a rich man's tomb (Isaiah 53:9). There was only one person who fits all of the messianic prophecies of the Old Testament: Jesus of Nazareth, the Son of Mary. In all, there are over three hundred prophecies that tell of the ancestry, birth, life, ministry, death, resurrection, and ascension of Jesus of Nazareth. All have been literally fulfilled to the smallest detail.

A fact often overlooked by critics is that, even if most biblical predictions could be explained naturally, the existence of just one real case of fulfilled prophecy is sufficient to establish the Bible's supernatural origin. Over 25 percent of the entire Bible contains specific predictive prophecies that have been literally fulfilled. This is true of no other book in the world. And it is a sure sign of its divine origin.[1]

Chapter Four

SALVATION IN CHRIST THE PROMISE OF HEAVEN AND ETERNAL LIFE

*"For what shall it profit a man,
if he shall gain the whole world, and lose his own soul?"*

—MARK 8:36

There are no words to describe the frustration of being a Christian. However, that frustration grows worse when dealing with atheists. Think about it. Creation testifies to an intelligent designer— a loving God. God, out of His own perfect and just righteousness and out of His love for us, demands a high moral standard: a moral standard that we constantly fail. When measured against God's Law, each one of us misses the mark. As mentioned before, history proves that we cannot save ourselves from our failures or from the punishment we richly deserve because of them.

Yet God, in His justice and holiness, cannot let our sins remain unpunished. More than that, because of His love for us, He hates it that sin separates us from Him. He knows even better than we how desperately we need saving, and the only One powerful enough to save us is the One Who created us in the first place. God, therefore, did the only thing He could do that would satisfy both His justice and

His love for us. In the Person of Jesus Christ, He took our sins upon Himself, thereby paying our debt and offering us a chance at salvation and a restored relationship with Him. It's all so profound, yet so simple at the same time. It seems so unbelievable, but it's the only thing that truly makes sense. And it's frustrating and heartbreaking when people can't or won't see it.

God offers everlasting life to all humanity through genuine repentance and a childlike faith in Jesus Christ. Everlasting life! Yet secular humanity doubts, ignores, and scoffs at God's promise of salvation from death and hell. The unspeakable frustration comes in knowing what they will miss (heaven) and what they will endure (hell). But the atheist goes one further than doubting the promises of God. He doubts the *existence* of God, in the stark face of a creation that proves *beyond a doubt* that there is a God.

Such craziness makes me want to throw up my hands in despair, and then wash them of anything to do with atheism. But I can't. Compassion won't let me. I thank God for the love and concern that He places in those who trust Him. Without it, I'm not sure I would even care about the salvation of anyone but myself and my immediate family and friends.

I would like to ask you a couple of relevant questions pertaining to the "sacrifice" of Jesus and its purpose. Please logically explain why an omnipotent, omniscient, and omni-benevolent God would need to sacrifice Himself (as Jesus) to Himself (God) in order to forgive man of sins against Him (God)? The entire premise seems totally absurd.

I appreciate the way you said that the sacrifice of the Cross *seems* absurd. It does. The Bible is in agreement with you: "For the message of the Cross is foolishness to those who are perishing, but to us who are being saved it is the power of God" (1 Corinthians 1:18). There's good reason that it seems absurd.

Imagine if I said to you, "I just sold my house, my car, and used all my savings to pay a fine for you." You would understandably think that I am rather weird. My paying a fine for you, when you don't think you have done anything wrong, is absurd.

But if I put it this way, it may make more sense: "Angry police officers showed up with a warrant for your arrest. They have video of you going eighty miles per hour through an area set aside for a blind children's convention. There were clear warning signs everywhere saying that fifteen miles per hour was the maximum speed. You are in big trouble. Add to that the fact that, just ten minutes prior to that happening, the police stopped you for drunk driving and confiscated your driver's license. You were in serious trouble with the law. The judge was furious, and handed down a massive fine. He said that if you couldn't pay it, you were going to be thrown in prison for a very long time. I knew you didn't have any money, so I sold my house, my car, and I used all my savings to pay that fine. You are free to go."

The reason you think the fine being paid for you two thousand years ago is absurd is because you don't realize that you have seriously broken the moral Law (the Ten Commandments) and you are in big trouble (see 1 John 3:4). In your drunken atheistic stupor you have ignored the clear warning signs of your violated conscience, and you have sped with reckless abandon into sin. All the while, the video has been rolling. God is omnipresent and omniscient. He has seen your lust (see Matthew 5:27-28), fornication, lies, anger, blasphemy, and rebellion. He sees your thought life and the darkness as if it were pure light (see Psalm 139:1-12). To say that He is angry at you is a massive understatement. His wrath abides on you (see John 3:36). You are His enemy (see James 4:4). Every time you sin against His Law, you are storing up His wrath (see Romans 2:5). Not believing that fact won't change a thing.

You could try to trivialize your crimes, but before you do, think of this. If I lied to my dog, it wouldn't be a big deal. If I was caught in a lie to my wife, I may have to spend the night on the couch. If I lied to my boss, I may lose my job. If I lied to a Supreme Court judge, I will spend a long time in prison. Even though it's the same crime, the penalty increases according to the importance of the one to whom I am lying.

All sin is against Almighty God (see Psalm 51:1-4). It is His Law that you have violated with your lust, lying, stealing, hatred, fornication, and blasphemy, etc. You are as guilty as sin, and what's more you cannot justify (make things right) yourself.

So, how can your fine be paid? How about you offer all the gold, all the diamonds, or all the oil in the world? That won't work. It all belongs to God anyway. You have nothing to offer God as a payment. Nothing.

Think of the ancient Aztecs. They could see that they had angered their dozens of gods (the evident suffering, disease, and death), so they would try to appease them with a "payment." They would take the most precious thing they had—a handsome youth or a beautiful virgin—and they would sacrifice it on a bloody altar to try to make atonement. However, the Bible says that any sacrifice we make is an abomination to God. He strictly forbids *human* sacrifice. You may remember that He tested Abraham's love for Him by telling him to offer his only son. As he was about to sacrifice Isaac, God stopped him and then He provided the sacrifice. This foreshadowed God sacrificing His only begotten Son for the sin of the world.

Besides being a murderous act, human sacrifice offers tainted sinful blood. It would be like me offering a judge drug money to pay your fine.

So what is precious enough to pay your fine and justify you so that you are free from the wrath of God's Law? Here's where the sacrifice makes sense.

As I have said, God Himself provided the sacrifice. Jesus was morally perfect. His blood wasn't tainted with sin like yours and mine—"…knowing that you were not redeemed with corruptible things, like silver or gold, from your aimless conduct received by tradition from your fathers, but with the precious blood of Christ, as of a lamb without blemish and without spot" (1 Peter 1:18-19). When He was on that terrible Cross, He was paying the fine for the Law that you and I violated (what love is that!).

Most people don't know that Jesus of Nazareth was Almighty God in human form. God prepared a body for Himself and filled that body as a hand fills a glove (see John 1:1, Colossians 1:15-16; 1 Timothy 3:16). The Creator was in Christ "reconciling the world to Himself."

One of the last things Jesus uttered on the Cross was, "It is finished!" The better Greek rendering is (English is inadequate) "The debt has been paid!" That now means that God can legally dismiss your case. He can commute your death sentence and let you live forever.

This was confirmed by the fact that God raised Jesus from the dead. It was God saying, "Humanity can now be justified."

This is why religious works (giving money to charities, praying five times a day, lying on beds of nails, or sitting on hard pews) cannot justify us. God will not be bribed (see Ephesians 2:8-9). The only thing that can save us from damnation (the just punishment for our sins) is the grace of God (unmerited favor— mercy from the judge), and that comes through repentance and faith (trust) alone in Jesus.

Some may ask why God didn't just simply forgive us. This is because He is *bound* by His own holy character. The Bible tells us that His Law is perfect, holy, just, and good. We are also told that *God* is perfect, holy, just, and good. So, we *cannot* separate God from His Law. It is His very essence. Scripture calls Him "the habitation of justice," and perfect justice *demands* retribution. That wrath-filled retribution fell on the Savior. If you refuse to repent, it will fall on you. Jesus warned that it would "grind to powder." When something is ground to powder, a *thorough* job is done. The Law will search out every sinful thought, word, and deed.

So there you have it. God loved you so much that He provided a sacrifice to save you from death and hell. Call upon Him today, and He will save you. You have His immutable promise: "For the message of the Cross is foolishness to those who are perishing, but to us who are being saved it is the power of God."

P.S. If it still seems absurd, read the last sentence through slowly, and try to figure out why.

I can find no reference to God not hearing our prayers, but to the contrary. Since we are born sinners and have to grow in our relationship with God through Christ, if He is not listening to our prayers from the beginning, then how can He forgive the sins that separate us from Him?

Here are two verses (there are others): "If I regard iniquity in my heart, the Lord will not hear me" (Psalm 66:18). "But your iniquities have separated between you and your God, and your sins have hid his face from you, *that he will not hear*" (Isaiah 59:2, italics added).

If we remain in rebellion to God, clinging to sin, He will take no notice of our prayers (obviously He is omniscient and "hears" all things). The Scriptures tell us that He "resists" the proud and gives grace to the humble. That's why a proud person can think that there is no God. He believes that his prayers didn't make it above the ceiling. And he is right. He needs to approach God in humility of heart. That way He will listen.

Look at Isaiah 66:2: "For all those things has my hand made, and all those things have been, says the Lord; but to this man will I look, even to him that is poor and of a contrite spirit, and trembles at my word." God takes notice of the humble prayer. He forgives sin and reveals Himself (in salvation), only when there is repentance and faith in Jesus.

Are you actually suggesting that these individuals can soften their own hearts? Are you suggesting that they can take a small step of faith which will somehow open the doors to God's saving grace?

Thanks for taking the time to share your concern. This is an issue with which I regularly wrestle—how do God's sovereign grace and man's responsibility to turn to Him fit together? For example, Ezekiel 33:11 says, "'As I live,' says the Lord God, 'I have no pleasure in the death of the wicked, but that the wicked turn from his way and live. Turn, turn from your evil ways! For why should you die...?'" God Himself tells the sinner to "turn" from his evil ways.

It is clear from Scripture that He gives us repentance (Acts 11:18; 2 Timothy 2:25), and He also gives us faith as a gift (Romans 12:3). But He then commands all men everywhere to repent and to have faith (believe) (see Mark 1:15; Acts 17:30).

Also, James 4:8 addresses sinners directly, telling them to draw near to God, cleanse their hands, and purify their hearts: "Draw near to God and He will draw near to you. Cleanse your hands, you sinners; and purify your hearts, you double-minded." Jesus rebuked His disciples and called them "foolish" because they didn't believe (Mark 16:14; Luke 24:25).

Charles Spurgeon proclaimed divine sovereignty and yet he also preached man's responsibility, although he admitted that he didn't understand how they fit together. Look at his exhortations to the sinner: "Believe in Jesus, and though you are now in slippery places your feet shall soon be set upon a rock of safety.... Sinner, fly to Christ."[1] "O sinner, humble yourself under the mighty hand of God..."[2] "Trust Christ with your soul and He will save it. I know you will not do this unless the Holy Spirit constrains you, but this does not remove your responsibility."[3]

Why can't God change gay people if they want to change?

If someone comes to God for the purpose of being "cured" of homosexuality, they are almost certain to end up worse than when they started. This is because no one should seek to become a Christian to have their problems fixed. The reason all should come to Christ is to be saved from sin—not from a problem or from a lifestyle they seek to change. This is the problem with the erroneous message of the modern church. It promises what it can't deliver. It says, "Problems? Come to Jesus. Something missing? Come to Jesus. Unhappy? Come to Jesus. Want to change? etc." Around 90 percent *who "come to Christ" for these reasons* fall away from the faith (my book *The Way of the Master* has two pages filled with examples of the 90 percent fall-away statistic).

The Bible puts it this way: "For if, after they have escaped the pollutions of the world through the knowledge of the Lord and Savior Jesus Christ, they are again entangled in them and overcome, the latter end is *worse* for them than the beginning" (2 Peter 2:20, italics added). Many of the skeptics who frequent my site had that experience, and that's why they are so bitter. I don't blame them. They heard a false gospel, had a false conversion, and justifiably feel duped—which they were.

No one should make a commitment to Christ because they want to "change." If they seek a change, they should go to Alcoholics

Anonymous, get on a daytime talk show for a makeover, or see a psychologist. But if they want everlasting life, they must repent of all sin (not just the ones of their choosing), and they must totally trust the Savior for their eternal salvation.

For all who come to Christ in true repentance and faith, God is able to change their sexual preference. Included in the list of those who won't inherit the kingdom of God are homosexuals (along with idolaters, adulterers, thieves, etc.). But Scripture goes on to say, "And such were some of you. But you were washed, but you were sanctified, but you were justified in the name of the Lord Jesus and by the Spirit of our God" (1 Corinthians 6:9-11). He puts a new spirit within them, and gives them a new heart with new desires. Thousands of ex-gays attest to the power of God to change lives.

Ray, why, then, did God make people homosexual? Isn't this cruel? I suppose you will say that they "choose" to be homosexual. I think you and I know this is absurd. Why then would God make them this way only to prohibit the strongest of all urges in people?

Good question. It's common for Christians to say that homosexuals weren't "born that way"—that they instead choose that lifestyle. I think we are all born "that way" because we inherit a sinful nature. I didn't have to teach my children to lie, to steal, to be selfish, etc. They naturally knew how to do that. I had to teach them to do what was right. As each of us grows from childhood, we have the potential to be a fornicator, a liar, a thief, an adulterer, a pervert, a homosexual, a drunkard, a murderer, a rapist, or a pedophile. So we didn't choose the sinful nature, but we did choose to follow a particular sin.

The good news is that God not only forgives sin, but He also gives us a new heart (a new inner self) that desires to do that which pleases Him—to do that which is right. Hopefully, if you are still in your sins, you will repent and trust the Savior before the Day of Judgment, when the door of mercy will close. After that happens, there won't be a hope in hell, so take sin seriously:

> Do you not know that the unrighteous will not inherit the
> kingdom of God? Do not be deceived. Neither fornicators, nor

idolaters, nor adulterers, nor homosexuals, nor sodomites, nor thieves, nor coveters, nor drunkards, nor revilers, nor extortionists will inherit the kingdom of God. And such were some of you. But you were washed, but you were sanctified, but you were justified in the name of the Lord Jesus and by the Spirit of our God (1 Corinthians 6:9-11).

THE PROMISE OF HEAVEN

I have a pretty good concept of what you think hell is, but no idea really about heaven. So, I have a request...could you describe heaven for us. What's that like? What goes on there? Where is it?

The concept of heaven is ridiculous. That's what I used to think. It wasn't the location that bothered me, it was the notion that it could be a reality. It couldn't work. This was my reasoning. A young couple is married. They love each other with a deep and undying love. He tragically dies a year after they are married, and goes to heaven to wait for her. She still loves him and remains faithful to him. She never remarries. Then she goes to be with him in heaven, when she's a senile and wrinkled ninety-eight-year-old. He wouldn't recognize her and she wouldn't remember him. The concept of heaven was nice, but in reality, seemed ridiculously impossible.

Then I came to know the Lord in 1972, and quickly changed my mind. Remember, that's why science changes its mind. It gets more information. I realized that if an invisible God could, in a moment of time, supernaturally change me into a new person, heaven could exist. If a man promises to give me ten million dollars, and freely gives me a million dollars as a token of good faith, he has proven himself to me to be utterly trustworthy. That's what God does. He gives those who obey Him the experience of new birth (the Holy Spirit) as a token of good faith. This is the teaching of the Bible: "He has also appropriated and acknowledged us as His by putting His seal upon us and giving us His Holy Spirit in our hearts as the security deposit and guarantee of the fulfillment of His promise" (2 Corinthians 1:22, *Amplified Bible*).

As science has discovered in the last couple of centuries, we are surrounded by invisible realms. Take for instance television or radio waves. We can't see them, but they are there whether we believe in them or not. We now understand that we need a "receiver."

It's the same with the spiritual realm. It, like television and radio waves, is invisible to the human eye. To experience the power of God we need a "receiver," and that receiver is unplugged until we are "born of the Spirit" (see John 3:1-5). That's why I thought Christianity was so foolish: "But the natural man does not receive the things of the Spirit of God, for they are foolishness to him; nor can he know them, because they are spiritually discerned" (1 Corinthians 2:14).

The location of heaven doesn't concern me. Just because I couldn't tell you the exact location of the country of Mauritania doesn't mean it doesn't exist.

Most people don't realize that the Bible teaches that heaven is coming down to Earth. This is despite the fact that daily millions pray "Thy Kingdom come. Thy will be done on Earth, as it is in Heaven." God is going to set up His kingdom on this earth. When it comes, He is going to remove the Genesis curse—that means that there will be no more floods, tornados, hurricanes, droughts, earthquakes, deserts, disease, weeds, pain, suffering, or death. It is then that the lion will lie down with the lamb. Creation will stop devouring itself (see Romans 8:18-25). Those who trust in Jesus Christ will be given brand new bodies that will be like the resurrected body of Jesus—bodies that can eat, touch, feel, etc., but will never age or feel pain or sorrow. This all sounds too good to be true, but it can be a proven reality for those who believe the Gospel.

Think of it—eternal life—on this wonderful earth restored to the purity of the Garden of Eden. A place where there are no rapists, no murderers, no pedophiles, no hypocrites, liars, blasphemers, or thieves. A place of perfect fruit, incredible animals, unimaginable color, massive waterfalls, amazing plants, more beautiful birds, bigger fish, grander canyons…and if you die in your sins, you are going to miss out and instead end up in hell—being punished for your sins, simply because of your prejudice and stubborn pride. What a tragedy.

One other thing. The Creator of the Universe—Almighty God (the One you don't believe in) will be there. He will say, "Behold I make all things new," and He doesn't need to use His past creation as a blueprint. He is the ultimate Creator with the ultimate creativity. Before this world existed as we know it, who could ever have imagined a blue sky, a brilliant sun, myriads of birds, gorgeous flowers, multitudes of colorful fish, deep blue seas, and an array of incredible animals? But this time, He will make all things new. Completely. We are waiting for a new heaven (sky) and a new earth (Isaiah 65:17; 1 Peter 3:13). We are also told that God will remove the sea (Revelation 21:1). Imagine that. That will give us a little more room.

Scripture tells us a number of times that "God is light." So there will be no longer a need for the sun, because He Himself will radiate in all of His unspeakable glory. Two thousand years ago He was manifest in human form to save us from death. However, Jesus of Nazareth is no longer the Man who was limited to time and space. He has ascended into heaven and is "glorified"—in the state that He was in before He came to this Earth. He now dwells in "light that is unapproachable," and shines "above the brightness of the sun."

Mere words could never express my infinite gratitude toward Him for giving me life, and then for saving me from being justly damned in hell for my sins. But I will have eternity to love and worship Him at whose right hand are "pleasures forevermore." No enjoyment on this sad old earth has come even close to the unending pleasures that God has prepared "for those that love Him." This is the teaching of the Bible. And you are going to miss out, simply because you refuse to change your mind, repent, and trust the Savior.

Two strikes against heaven for me. No seas, no seafood. He would give me a perfect body then take away lust. That's just cruel.

As one who doesn't believe in God, you are perhaps mocking, but I will address the thought anyway. When the Bible says that there will be no more sea on the new earth, it doesn't say that there will be no more water. I can't say for sure but there may be beautiful lakes, teeming with succulent fish. After the resurrection, Jesus was in His resurrected body and prepared and (presumably) ate fish with His disciples (see John 21:9-13).

Your words reveal that, like most normal males, you live for sexual lust. It gives your sinful heart great pleasure, and you can't think of a life without lusting for women. However, the miracle of conversion is that God takes our wicked and perverted hearts and gives us new desires. You are forgetting Who made women in the first place. It was God. What you see in the beauty of a woman isn't a glorified primate.

As Christians, we are still tempted by the pleasure of lust, but we now know better. We now know that God sees lust as adultery, and He warns that those who give themselves to sexual perversion (lust) will end up in hell.

When a sinner is born again, God washes away all of his sins. He is forgiven every perverted sexual thought and granted the gift of eternal life. What a fool he would be to give up his eternal salvation (eternal life) for the fleeting pleasures of lust.

Maybe I'm not impressed by the offer because I'm almost completely satisfied with the world as it is, and would only ask for changes that involve people taking better care of what they have. I don't want a new earth, thank you. I want the one we already live on, and I just want people to be more careful with it. So far, the impression I get from Ray is that he doesn't care about the gift of the world that his God gave us—he and other Christians have admitted that by saying things like "why bother cleaning up the planet when we're just going to get a new one, anyway?"

Did you say that you don't want a new earth, and that you just want people to more careful with the one we have? Okay, let's be careful with what we do with plastic, etc. Now, how do we stop earthquakes, hurricanes, tsunamis, tornadoes, floods, famines, draughts, disease, pollution, untold suffering, and ultimate death? Let me know if you have a plan.

Then you say "the impression I get from Ray is that he doesn't care about the gift of the world that his God gave us." I care. I don't throw trash on the ground. I often pick it up. I hate graffiti. I have a vegetable garden and a chicken coop. I ride a bike to and from work (what do you drive?). I eat organic cereal, and I like trees. I don't tie myself to them (I live in California—fourteen hundred wildfires). But I have to add that I think they are great for making houses.

Frankly, I don't think that you think I don't care about God's earth. You are just upset that you have no answer to that picture I posted of His incredible handiwork. You had better get right with Him, or you will not only miss out on "pleasures forevermore," but you will reap the full consequences of your sin. All we can do is warn you. The rest is up to you.

If "salvation" is a "supernatural" act of a "supernatural God," then evangelism would be superfluous, no?

The Armenian and Calvinist views are diametrically opposed to each other, yet believers on both sides point to a thousand scriptures to back their theology. If you choose one view or the other, don't let your choice cut you off from others who may believe differently. The two opposing truths can walk together. All that's missing is some information for them to harmonize. The day will come when we will understand everything (1 Corinthians 13:12), and we will be glad that we didn't cause division by arguing about which one is right.

Sadly, church history has shown us that Christ-centered men of God have clashed over these issues (e.g., Wesley and Whitefield). More recently, I have seen brethren make a theological stand and much to their dismay, they were marked by their home church as "troublemakers." Fine missionaries have been pulled from the field, pastors fired from the ministry, and churches have split, simply because of different views of God's sovereignty.

So, if you do get it worked out, be careful that you strive to keep unity among the brethren, and then focus on your God-given commission. Firefighters exist to fight fires, not to fight each other. They must have unity of purpose.

Every moment that you and I spend arguing about theological interpretations is time we have lost forever, that could have been spent in prayer for the unsaved or in seeking to save that which is lost.

Chapter Five

THE TESTIMONY
OF HOLY SCRIPTURE

"I have a fundamental belief in the Bible as the Word of God, written by
men who were inspired. I study the Bible daily. Opposition to godliness is
atheism in profession and idolatry in practice. Atheism is so senseless and
odious to mankind that it never had many professors."[1]

—SIR ISAAC NEWTON

Recently an atheist asked if he could interview me on video for his "Backyard Skeptics" ministry. He began with a few general questions, and then he said, "Let's see some of those funny pictures in your wallet." He knew that my wallet contains a few humorous photos (my ID has a picture of me with a large stretched forehead). I kindly obliged. But instead of showing his audience the pictures, he immediately positioned the wallet toward the camera and said, "Let's see how much money an evangelist carries in his wallet." Unfortunately for him, the portion in which he looked contained more humorous material— a genuine shrunken one dollar bill, and a three and a four dollar bill. He was obviously disappointed that I didn't have a wad of one hundreds. His attempt at exposé journalism kind of flopped.

Sadly, the hypocrisy of money-hungry televangelism has marred Christianity and made it difficult to hold on to credibility with an already doubting world. It was this same committed atheist who gave me a sheet of paper that listed his problems with the Bible. Heading the list was 1 Corinthians 1:26, a verse which he said proved that atheists are smarter than Christians.

Here is the verse: "For you see your calling, brethren, how that not many wise men after the flesh, not many mighty, not many noble, are called." He seemed to have skipped over the words "after the flesh." There are different types of wisdom. There is the wisdom of this world ("after the flesh"), and there is the wisdom of God. The message of the passage is that God has chosen a seemingly foolish message of childlike faith, to confound those proud folks who think that they are wise.

So, if you look around the Christian faith, you won't find many of those proud people who are puffed up in their own "fleshly" wisdom. So the atheist isn't wiser than the dumbest of Christians. Rather, according to the Bible, he or she is a fool (see Psalm 14:1).

Also on the list was a reference to Japheth, saying that he sacrificed his daughter. Somehow my atheist friend (and he is a friend) thought that, because the Bible related the incident it was somehow condoning it. He looked a little taken aback when I told him that Japheth was lacking in intellectual capacity. What Japheth did was stupid.

The Scriptures are given to us for our instruction. We can learn life lessons from all the stupid things that men and women did in the Bible. Noah became drunk and shamed himself. Saul became jealous and destroyed his life. Judas was a hypocrite and ended up killing himself. Peter slept when he should have been in prayer, and denied his Lord. David let lust into his heart, and committed adultery, then murder. These incidents were written for our admonition, and we can either humbly learn from them or proudly walk down the same tragic path. The choice is ours.

So God doesn't like smart people? The thoughts of the wise are worthless…that's flirting with contradiction. The unavoidable implication is that God likes 'em dumb and ignorant.

It's important to read the Bible in context. First Corinthians 3:18 is speaking of anyone who "seems to be wise in this age," and goes on to explain that "the wisdom of this world is foolishness with God." Again, this is referring to those who are wise in their own eyes—they only think they are wise.

However, if you want to interpret the fact that not many wise people come to Christ because "God likes 'em dumb and ignorant," go ahead.

But let me see if you are a "wise" person. Can you make honey, from nothing? How about a glass of milk, from nothing? How about a living leaf? Can you make a living frog, or a cat, a horse or a cow, from nothing? How about an eye? Make me a fully functioning eye, using no materials. Can you? Of course you can't. You don't even have an intelligent answer to how those came about. You would probably say that evolution is responsible for making everything, but that it didn't make it from nothing. It made it from gases in space. Then where did the gases come from? You have to keep saying that there was something in the beginning, because basic science says that nothing can come from nothing.

Yep, you can't make a piece of sand from nothing. You don't know where we came from, why you are here, or what's going to happen after you die. You don't know much at all. So, if it's true that "God likes 'em dumb and ignorant," you sure qualify to be liked by Him.

Instead of being "dumb and ignorant," be wise. Listen to your conscience, acknowledge your many sins, and you will come to understand that God doesn't just *like* us "dumb and ignorant" people, He proved His great *love* for us, in that while we were yet sinners Christ died for us.

The Bible itself is presumed to be the Word of God written down by inspired men simply because the men said they were inspired? Or is there something else? Also, if the entire Bible, OT and NT, are to be the inerrant Word, how are differences between the OT and NT reconciled?

You have asked only two of a thousand questions you could ask about the Bible. However, its claim is summed up in that humanity has violated the Law of a holy God. He sees lust as adultery and hatred as murder. Lying lips are an abomination to Him. Death and then damnation in hell are our just (right) punishment for our crimes against Him. But God is rich in mercy and has paid the fine for the Law we violated through the suffering death of the Savior. Upon our repentance and faith alone in Jesus, God justifies us (makes us right with Him) and dismisses our case. He commutes our death sentence and lets us live—He freely gives us the gift of everlasting life. That's the Gospel, and if it's true, then it is the most incredible news that humanity could ever hope to hear.

If I picked up an instruction book that claimed to be for a certain appliance, how can I best prove what it says? I test its claims. The book says to plug the appliance in. I do that. It says to program it by flicking the left switch upwards. That will make a green light flash. It does. Now it says the right switch will make a red light flash. That happens too. It tells me to push the middle button three times and that will give me a picture. The picture comes on. It then tells me how to adjust the picture. I follow another twelve specific instructions from the book and watch the appliance do everything the book said it would. Logic tells me that this instruction book is the right book for that appliance. Any other conclusion would be lunacy.

This is the claim of the Instruction Book: "He who has My commandments and keeps them, it is he who loves Me. And he who loves Me will be loved by My Father, and I will love him and manifest [reveal] Myself to him" (John 14:21). Either that's true, or it isn't. If you are sincere in seeking the truth, then do what the Book says. Simply get on your knees, confess and forsake your beloved sins, and trust in Jesus for your eternal salvation. The light will come on. You will come to know God, you will pass from death to life, and you will pass from darkness to light. And then you will have a lot more questions. But they will be asked in humble awe.

How do you respond to a person when they say the Bible was written by a bunch of crazy people and you have to be crazy to believe it?

I would say, "Let's not argue about the inspiration of the Bible for a moment," and then I would take him through the Commandments. Jesus didn't say, "Go into all the world and convince people that the Bible is the Word of God." It is the *Gospel* that is the power of God for salvation, and the way to give the arrow of the Gospel its thrust is to put it into the bow of the Law.

We often hear that Christianity stands or falls on the validity of Scripture. I respectfully disagree. I believe the Bible is God's Word. There's no argument there. But my salvation isn't dependent upon that fact, because I wasn't converted by the Bible. I was converted by the power of God, and when I picked up a Bible it simply explained what had happened to me.

In our sincere efforts to convince a sinful world, we tend to use intellectual arguments (I'm often guilty of this), when the ultimate proof is the power of God transforming the human heart. But I didn't come to Christ through an intellectual argument, and my faith doesn't stand on human wisdom, so why should I try to bring others through that door?

If the whole scientific world came together and "disproved" the Bible, and archeologists found what were "proved" to be the bones of Jesus, it wouldn't shake my faith in the slightest. Not at all. This is what Paul speaks about in 1 Corinthians 2:4-5 when he says that the Christian's faith doesn't stand "in the wisdom of men, but in the power of God."

Remember, early Christians weren't converted by the Scriptures. Instead, they were saved by a *spoken* message. Most couldn't read anyway. The New Testament hadn't been compiled. There was no such thing as the printing press.

If you believe that our foundation for the faith is the written Scriptures rather than the person of Jesus Christ, I have some questions for you. When did Christianity begin? Was it on the Day of Pentecost when the three thousand were converted by the power of God, or did it have to wait until the New Testament was compiled in AD 200?

So don't feel that it's your mandate to convince anyone of the inspiration of the Word of God. You will never do it while they love their sins. For every reasonable argument you come up with, he will come back with a hundred and one atrocities and injustices in the Bible.

Instead, give the arrow of the Gospel thrust by using the Law of God to bring the knowledge of sin. Make the sinner thirst after a righteousness without which he will perish. Then, once he is born again and comes to know the Lord, the Scriptures will open up to him. Until that time, the things of God will seem foolishness to him, as the Scriptures say.

Congratulations, you have achieved at least one of your aims. As a result of your polemical postings, I have been reading more about the Bible in the last few weeks than I have probably ever done in my life. Some of it has been quite fascinating. Don't get too worked up about it. I am still an atheist. I have been reading quite a lot of documentation about the latest biblical research, though I confess purely from a historical/anthropological point of view. Interesting stuff all the same.

May I suggest that you also read the Bible itself? It's good that you are studying documentation, but other resources are the mere shadow of the reality. It would be wonderful if you could especially study the Gospel of John.

There are two ways you can read the Bible. One is with the light off. By that I mean that you read it with a proud heart, looking for mistakes, marking seeming contradictions, believing that you are intellectually superior to what you are reading.

The second way is with the light on. By that I mean with a humble heart, believing that you don't know everything, and that you could gain knowledge by studying the world's greatest-selling book of all time.

Read slowly, with a pen in your hand and underline the things said about Jesus of Nazareth—that all things were made by Him, that He was the very source of life in human form, why He came to this earth, etc. Then underline and ponder what He said about Himself—how He was preexistent, how He maintained that He was life itself, the conqueror of death, the sole way to immortality, and how He came specifically to suffer and die for our sins, then rise again. Take special note that He promises to manifest Himself to all who do what He says (see John 14:21). Either that's true or it's not.

The implications of such honest research are either frightening or they are unspeakably exhilarating, depending on your perspective.

Didn't Jesus say that it's impossible for a rich man to enter heaven?

Yes, He did.

> Then Jesus said to His disciples, "Assuredly, I say to you that it is hard for a rich man to enter the kingdom of heaven. And again I say to you, it is easier for a camel to go through the eye of a needle than for a rich man to enter the kingdom of God." When His disciples heard it, they were greatly astonished, saying, "Who then can be saved?" But Jesus looked at them and said to them, "With men this is impossible, but with God all things are possible" (Matthew 19:23-26).

Then Scripture goes on to tell of a rich man entering the kingdom of heaven (see Luke 19:1). A man named Zacchaeus, whom the Scriptures say was rich, humbled himself and surrendered to Christ. Then Jesus said, "Today salvation has come to this house" (verse 9). So if you are rich, make sure that you love God more than you love your money, and hold onto it with a loose hand.

Let me try and understand this. According to you, Jesus DID say that it's impossible for a rich man to enter heaven. Then down in the very same post you describe a rich man who did what Jesus said is impossible. Now explain to me again how there are no internal contradictions in the Bible?

There is no contradiction. This is what the Bible says:

> Then Jesus looked around and said to His disciples, "How hard it is for those who have riches to enter the kingdom of God!" And the disciples were astonished at His words. But Jesus answered again and said to them, "Children, how hard it is for those who trust in riches to enter the kingdom of God! It is easier for a camel to go through the eye of a needle than for a rich man to enter the kingdom of God." And they were greatly astonished, saying among themselves, "Who then can be saved?" But Jesus looked at them and said, "With men it is impossible, but not with God; for with God all things are possible" (Mark 10:23-27).

We are told that the disciples were "astonished" at what He said. So it seems that Jesus was talking about a literal camel and a literal needle—something truly impossible. But then Jesus added that with God nothing is impossible. That means that He can change the money-loving heart of a rich man if He so desires.

The fact is, it's "impossible" for *anyone* to enter the kingdom of God without the help of God. No amount of riches can buy your way in. The Bible says that there are "none" who seek after God (see Romans 3:10-12). We hate God without cause. His name is used as a cuss word, and some even do the unthinkable—they deny that He exists, which is extremely foolish in the face of this incredible creation. So, it takes what is called "grace" to draw us to Him. He softens the hardened heart, opens the closed mind, and changes our wrong direction. He then opens our blind eyes and gives us light so that we can understand the Gospel and be saved. This is described in detail in 2 Corinthians 4:3-6. God did this with me, and He can do it with you—if you are willing. Amazing grace.

What's the verse that says "love" of money is the root of all evil?

This is one of the most misquoted verses in the Bible. Typically, Hollywood has passed the buck and blamed *money* as being evil rather than humanity. However, the buck stops at man, not money. It's not lucre that's filthy.

Scripture says, "But those who desire to be rich fall into temptation and a snare, and into many foolish and harmful lusts which drown men in destruction and perdition. For the love of money is a root of all kinds of evil, for which some have strayed from the faith in their greediness, and pierced themselves through with many sorrows" (1 Timothy 6:9-11).

So, a talking snake, a man living in a whale's stomach for three days, a virgin pregnancy, and a man walking on water don't contradict logic?

So, a talking parrot, three hundred people flying through the sky in a big tin can called a 747, a human being growing inside another person, and men walking on the moon don't contradict logic? Of course they do, if you are small-minded. However, science and technology have exploded the word. It has a completely different meaning than it had one hundred years ago.

Small-minded people are limited by the confines of what they see as logic. However, when we are born again, the supernatural takes logic into a new realm. When we discover that the supernatural is a reality our mind is suddenly expanded and logic explodes.

Animals could easily talk—if the supernatural is involved. After all, speech is merely thought manifesting as sound, and who would deny that animals think? A man could easily live in the stomach of a whale (or "great fish") if it was "prepared" by the God who made it, as the Bible says it was. A virgin could easily become pregnant if the One who made the virgin was involved. And walking on water is a breeze...when God is manifest in human form.

Why does the Bible compare us to pigs?

It would seem that in our day of political correctness, it flies in the face of some to use even famous metaphors, such as Jesus' admonition not to "cast your pearls before swine" (Matthew 7:6). But our culture is filled with metaphors, similes, and colloquialisms. For instance, consider this example: "I took my wife to a restaurant the other day. Man, you pay through the nose at that place! I left feeling down in the mouth." Taken literally, the imagery is disgusting. However, to the metaphor-savvy, it simply means that the restaurant was so expensive, it left me depressed.

So, when I borrow the biblical expression "casting pearls before swine" in reference to atheists rejecting the Gospel, I don't mean that I am literally casting precious pearls to pigs. It is metaphoric, meaning that the Gospel is the offer of eternal life—immortality, absolute and complete victory over death. There could be nothing more precious, so it is likened to valuable pearls. Think now of swine and their attitude toward the precious nature of pearls. The pigs couldn't care less about them. Their only concern is their appetite for unclean things, for the filth in which they wallow to satisfy their flesh. Yep, perfect analogy. The Bible takes the cake. It hits the nail on the head. By the way, never mix your metaphors.

Chapter Six

WHAT SETS CHRISTIANITY AND CHRISTIANS APART?

Nor is there salvation in any other,
for there is no other name under heaven
given among men by which we must be saved."

—ACTS 4:12 (*NKJV*)

I *never give up trying to reach atheists.* There is hope while there is breath in their lungs. This offends many Christians who have told me not to "cast my pearls before swine." They know that many with whom I speak are bitter and angry and might mock the name of Christ or reject the Gospel. But I sympathize with nonbelievers because some know nothing of *genuine* Christianity. All they have seen is the inside of a dead Catholic church or the hypocrisy of the money-hungry "prosperity gospel" version of Christianity we find all over the airwaves and all across bookstore shelves today.

I can't help but think that every bitter and angry atheist may have a praying mother, brother, or sister pleading with God for someone to speak the truth in love to their precious relative—for a genuine Christian to provide a living testimony to the truth and power of the Gospel.

Before Kirk Cameron and I debated two bitter atheists on ABC's *Nightline*, the mother of one wrote to me and sincerely thanked me for befriending her beloved son. She was a Christian and she believed that the contact we were having with him prior to the debate was an answer to prayer.

Immediately before the debate itself, a woman in the front row introduced herself to me. She was the mother of the other bitter atheist. She also loved the Lord and thanked us for befriending her daughter. The sister of the atheist who videotaped my wallet was also a Christian, and she wrote to thank me for befriending her beloved brother. So I will keep casting the pearls of biblical truth, and leave where they land up to God.

How do you know you have the right God?

Good question. There are many religions and many ways that are said to lead to God, so how do we Christians know that we have the right one? There are ancient Greek and Roman gods. There is the Aztec god. There's the god of the Mormons. He lives on a distant planet with a number of wives, making spirit babies to populate other planets, and we can become gods like him if we

---

Hope for a "True Atheist"

"I was a true atheist, addicted to pornography and a big fan of torture. I hated the Bible and literally looked at 'contract killer' as a career option. I favored Darwinian abortion of potentially disabled children and agreed with the majority of Adolph Hitler's statements about the disabled and invalid. I fantasized about murder and contemplated suicide and held nothing but hatred in my heart for anyone who told me I was wrong. In short, I was the most degenerate scum to ever walk the Earth. That God saved me is still so far beyond my comprehension I have to wake up every day and think 'wow.'

"Nowadays, I work at the church I once hated going to. I greet daily a pastor I once did everything in my power to ignore, and I serve as an assistant to a youth leader I once despised. I play in the Sunday band and teach drums to young boys of the congregation for extra income. I teach Sunday school and am a regular fixture at the weekly prayer meetings and church events.

People who have known me throughout the process have told me how astonishing it is to have seen the transformation. But no one is as impressed as me with how God has changed my heart and my life.

"So, that's me. I'm a 6'6," nineteen-year-old motorcyclist who plays drums, carries a Bible, vacuums a church, writes scripts that will never be made into films, and carries around a hefty supply of the *Way of the Master* on his iPod." —Jacques Reulet

do what the Mormon religion requires. Then there is the buffet god—the god of Oprah. You pick and choose what you like from all the religions, and then create a god in your own image, one that suits you. Then again, you could make evolution your god, and give it praise for creating everything through (super)natural selection. You could even see yourself as god. Many do. The God of the Hebrews said, "You shall have no other gods before Me" (Exodus 20:3). That God maintains that we are directly responsible to Him for our thoughts, words, and deeds.

The prophets of a god named Baal believed that he was God, the Creator. Elijah, a Hebrew prophet, said that he wasn't. So they built separate altars, and Elijah said that whoever answered by fire would be the one true God. The prophets of Baal prayed their hearts out and nothing happened. Elijah prayed, and fire fell from the heavens and burned up his sacrifice completely. There was nothing left (see 1 Kings 18:20-40).

Here's how you can know the right way. You have a dilemma that is even greater than the one you think you have of not knowing which is the right God. It's the dilemma of "guilt." Everyone has it. You can drown it in booze or say it doesn't exist, or insist that you don't feel guilt, but it is still something you have. This is because it's not a feeling; it's a condition.

Let's look at one of the Ten Commandments to see what I mean. "You have heard that it was said to those of old, 'You shall not commit adultery.' But I say to you that whoever looks at a woman to lust for her has already committed adultery with her in his heart" (Matthew 5:27-28). Are you guilty? Of course you are. Lust leaves us all guilty. We lust sexually, and whether we believe it or not, we are going to stand before the Creator and give an account of ourselves, right down to the sexual imagination of the heart.

The conscience produces guilt, and guilt produces fear of impending judgment. We can say, "I don't believe that," but our unbelief doesn't erase the guilt. Nor can it erase the reality of the impending judgment of hell. It's still there.

In comes the Gospel. It says that Jesus Christ suffered and died to take away my sin and my guilt. He came to erase it completely. The Gospel explains that a legal transaction took place between the

Creator and humanity two thousand years ago, through the suffering, death, and resurrection of Jesus Christ. I violated the moral Law of the Creator, and Jesus paid my fine so that my case could legally be dismissed.

Here's the promise of the Gospel. Upon my repentance and faith in Jesus, my guilt will disappear. All of it. Not for lust only, but for all of my sins—for ingratitude, rebellion, greed, unbelief, lying, stealing, fornication, etc. All the guilt disappears upon repentance and faith in Jesus. Oprah can't do that. The great religions can't do that. Neither can Mormonism. No other god can wash away my sins, because no other god answered by the fire of His wrath and consumed the sacrifice. That happened two thousand years ago when Christ died on the Cross. God accepted His sacrifice.

All manmade religions still offer sacrifices. That's the altar upon which they are built—the sacrifice of prayer, of giving money, of giving time, of doing good works, of doing penance, of fasting, etc. They have to sacrifice, because they still have guilt, because the conscience demands a continual sacrifice. Not so with Christianity. The guilt is removed because the sacrifice was accepted. Completely. And our guilt is dismissed through simple repentance and faith in Jesus. (Again, I'm not talking about a sense of guilt, but our actual condition—we're no longer lawbreaking criminals before a holy God.) It's so simple a child can understand it. Obey the Gospel, and the guilt is replaced by absolute assurance of everlasting life. Death loses its sting…"and you shall know the truth, and the truth shall make you free" (John 8:32).

I can't puzzle out how you can so easily dismiss other religions and their gods but find it impossible to do the same with your own. Almost all other religions have their holy books, their devoted followers, and the same certainty that they are correct and everyone else is wrong. What makes your certainty different from theirs? What makes your faith correct while theirs suffers from some obvious fallacy? Why are your sound arguments against the other gods and religions somehow not valid when applied to Christianity? What sets Christianity apart?

That is a very good question. Here's the answer in a nutshell. All "religions" are manmade, and they are based on something called "self-righteousness." They say that there are certain "things" (righteous deeds) that each of us must do to get to heaven and to escape hell. Muslims say that you must pray five times a day, fast, accept Mohammed as a prophet, etc. Hindus say you must do things to try to escape the hopeless spiral of reincarnation. Mormons and Jehovah's Witnesses say the same thing. They say that man's salvation is based on what he does. The reason they believe that is because they are ignorant of the standard that God requires of them. They think His standard of righteousness is the same as theirs. It's not. God's standard is absolute perfection, in thought, word, and deed. He considers lust as adultery, hatred as murder. Lying lips are "an abomination" to Him. He is so holy that His justice requires that all liars will have their part in the lake of fire. It is only when His Law comes into play (the Ten Commandments) that we begin to understand that we are desperately wicked criminals in His sight. We are standing guilty in the courtroom of eternal justice. It is the Law that shows us that our "good works" (religious deeds) are in truth attempts to bribe the Judge of the Universe, and that the catalyst of religious works is a guilty conscience, or what the Bible calls an "evil" conscience. However, God will not be bribed. We are guilty criminals against God, lawbreakers, and we await capital punishment. But the Bible tells us that this perfect and holy Judge of the Universe is "rich in mercy." If we fling ourselves on the mercy of the Court (through repentance and faith in Jesus), God can dismiss our case and let us live. He can commute our death sentence and save us from damnation in hell. And he can do that because He paid the fine for us in the life's blood of His Son. The Living God created for Himself a perfect body and filled that body as a hand fills a glove. Jesus of Nazareth was the "express image of the invisible God." He came to suffer and die in our place; to take the punishment for our sins. He came to pay our fine and defeat death. That's what separates Christianity from manmade religions. This is explained a little more clearly in my booklet, *Why Christianity?*[1]

Ray, I thought I'd share some facts with you. I just reviewed the FBI crime index, the teen pregnancy index, index of religion in the states, and index for each different religion in the states for 2007. The funny thing I found was that crime and violent crime rated highest in the most religious parts of America. Teen pregnancy did the same. The most concentrated area in America for both was not only the most religious portion of our nation but also where Baptist was the leading church body. The less religious and more secular areas' rates were significantly less in all categories mentioned. So if people choose to not believe in God so they can do all the horrible things his rules tell us not to do, why isn't the less religious portion of the American population doing them? Just curious. Does this prove there is a correlation between religion, crime, and teen pregnancy? Since this was just a quick run through with only a few sources used, I'd say no, but it really makes me wonder. It also greatly helps to refute some of your claims about those who reject your God.

This is a good question, and it brings out the essence of what our ministry teaches. The modern church has proclaimed a false gospel that has produced millions of false converts (those we commonly call "backsliders"). Do a little study among your atheist friends, and you will find that many are in this category. These people are normally bitter at Christianity. They feel cheated; and so they should. They heard a false gospel, and had a false conversion, and the Bible warns that those who experience such will end up in a worse state than before their so-called "conversion."

However, even more tragic than the creation of false converts who fall away from the faith is the category of false converts who stay within the Church. They profess the Christian faith, but as your statistics confirm, their hypocritical lifestyles don't match what they profess. The Bible calls them "goats" among the "sheep." In the Middle East it's extremely difficult to discern goats from sheep as they flock together. However, a good shepherd can tell the difference. The day will come when the Good Shepherd will separate the sheep from the goats. The sheep (the true converts) will go into everlasting life, and the goats (the false converts) will go into everlasting damnation.

Here is the difference between the true Gospel and the false gospel. The false message says that you should come to Christ "because something is missing in your life—you have a God-shaped hole in your heart. God has a wonderful plan for your life." But there is no biblical precedent for a message of life improvement upon conversion. None. In fact, the Bible says that you will have trials, tribulations, temptations, and persecution.

The reason any of us should come to Christ is because we are deceitfully wicked sinners, and we desperately need a Savior. Without the mercy of God in Christ, we will come under God's just wrath, and end up in hell. We should come to Christ for no other reason.

The false message is very popular for obvious reasons, and that's why popular preachers who preach the false gospel have such large followings. However, some people (like yourself), are beginning to see the discrepancy and asking why. It's our earnest prayer that they listen to what we are saying, and reform the message that's being preached.

If I become a believer in the divine, it will be a la *Anthony Flew. I'll never accept Christianity; sorry. I could never worship a God that could quite possibly be torturing Anne Frank.*

It seems that this skeptic is willing to believe in a God who created all things, but he's not willing to believe in a God who is a God of justice. His inference is that Anne Frank suffered enough without being punished by God for her sins.

Let's forget about what is commonly called "the age of accountability," and rather imagine that perhaps Anne heard the Gospel from those with whom she was captive in Nazi Germany, and as a Jew she embraced the Jewish Messiah. Then our skeptic friend will therefore end up in hell, when he could have instead ended up in heaven with Anne Frank. Let me continue to address this thought by quoting something I wrote in *The Evidence Bible:*

> In January 2000, a well-known ex-televangelist said on a worldwide TV talk show, "I believe that every person who died in the Holocaust went to heaven." He was very sincere, and if he was seeking the commendation of the world, he surely got it with that statement. Who wouldn't consider what

he said to be utterly compassionate? However, let's look at the implications of his heartfelt beliefs.

His statement seemed to limit salvation to the Jews who died in the Holocaust, because he added that "their blood laid a foundation for the nation of Israel." If the slaughtered Jews made it to heaven, did the many Gypsies who died in the Holocaust also obtain eternal salvation? If his statement includes Gentiles, is the salvation he spoke of limited to those who died at the hands of Nazis? Did the many Frenchmen who met their death at the hands of cruel Nazis go to heaven also?

Perhaps he was saying that the death of Jesus on the Cross covered all of humanity, and that all will eventually be saved— something called "universalism." This means that salvation will also come to Hitler and the Nazis who killed the Jews. However, I doubt if he was saying that. Such a statement would have brought the scorn of his Jewish host, and of the world whose compassion has definite limits. If pressed, he probably didn't mean that only the Jews in the camps went to heaven, because that smacks of racism. He was likely saying that those who died were saved because they died in such tragic circumstances.

Then Jesus was lying when He said, "I am the way, the truth, and the life: no man comes to the Father, but by me" (John 14:6). So, there is another way to heaven—death in a Nazi concentration camp? Does that mean that the many Jews who died under communism went to heaven? Or is salvation limited to German concentration camps? If their salvation came because of the grim circumstances surrounding their death, does a Jew therefore enter heaven after suffering for hours before dying in a car wreck…if he was killed by a drunk driver who happened to be German? Bear in mind that his suffering may have been much greater than someone who died within minutes in a Nazi gas chamber.

Many unsaved think we can merit entrance into heaven by our suffering. Their error was confirmed by this sincere, compassionate man of God. They may now disregard the truth, "Neither is there salvation in any other: for there is no other name under heaven given among men, whereby we must be saved" (Acts 4:12). They can now save themselves by the means of their own death…if they suffer enough. The ex-televangelist was concerned that his indiscretions of the 1980s brought discredit to the kingdom of God. However, those actions fade into history compared to the damage

> done by saying that there is another means of salvation outside of
> Jesus Christ, on a program watched by untold millions around the
> world. Who on earth needs to repent and trust in Jesus, if millions
> entered the kingdom without being born again? No one.[2]

I'm a little weary of hearing atheists parrot their popular and old
phrase about "God torturing His children," presumably speaking
of God sending sinners to hell.

There are two important truths to understand here. First: God
will not "torture" anyone. He will give them "justice." A criminal
may believe that his being thrown into a cold prison because he
viciously raped three teenage girls, is torture. The judge rather
knows better. He calls it "justice."

God will "damn" rebellious sinners from all that is good in a
prison called hell. He gave them life and lavished His goodness
upon them, and they despised Him and refused His mercy. So they
will get what the Bible calls "equity." Equity, according to the
dictionary, is "the quality of being fair or impartial; fairness;
impartiality: the equity of Solomon." In law, it is "the application of
the dictates of conscience or the principles of natural justice to the
settlement of controversies." In other words, impartially doing that
which is right, fair, and just.

Sinners are not God's children. The Bible makes that clear. We
are children of Satan, and it's his will we gladly run to do. Isn't it true
that we love the darkness and hate the light (see John 3:19)? We are
not His children until we are washed from our sins by the grace of
God, and are born of His Spirit through the new birth of John 3:1-5.

*Imagine if you are a scientific illiterate, a hack actor, inept at argument and
rhetoric, lacking imagination...Along comes this religion that suddenly
tells you that you're not a loser, and that you can be better than anyone else,
and all you have to do is believe in this Messiah.*

May I say with all due respect, you have confused the modern
message of the contemporary church with the one given by the Bible.
The message of Christianity isn't for those who have problems. That's
a common fallacy. It is true we are all in a sense losers, but not in the
way of which you are speaking. You and I are losers because our heart
is deceitfully wicked, and because God's wrath abides on us until we

repent and trust the Savior. If that's not enough for you, here's the Scriptures describing the moral state of humanity:

> There is none righteous, no, not one; there is none who understands; there is none who seeks after God. They have all turned aside; they have together become unprofitable; there is none who does good, no, not one. Their throat is an open tomb; with their tongues they have practiced deceit; the poison of asps is under their lips; whose mouth is full of cursing and bitterness. Their feet are swift to shed blood; destruction and misery are in their ways; and the way of peace they have not known. There is no fear of God before their eyes (Romans 3:11-18).

So you get your philosophy about not being a loser from the Bible. We are all big-time losers and jerks.

You have more than likely formulated your "problem people" thoughts from the message of contemporary televangelists, who, in the name of God, deceive the minds of the simple. They sell them holy water and pieces of holy material, and tell them that God wants them to be winners and to prosper, if they will just send in their seed money.

However, the true message of Christianity isn't just for those who have problems. It's also for those without problems. It's a universal message. It's also for those who are happily enjoying their fornication and pornography. It's for both rich and poor, top rockers and rock bottomers, happy and sad—all of us need God's mercy, which is available only in Jesus Christ.

THE TESTIMONY OF GENUINE CHRISTIANS

I think that whether the scriptures are true or not is irrelevant. Christianity is a mindset, a philosophy, a way of living, that depends on the practitioners/believers practicing it more than anything...When I was a Christian...

It's important to speak truthfully about our experiences, by using the correct terminology. Rather than saying "When I was a Christian," you should say "When I professed to be a Christian," or, to be biblically sound, "When I was a false convert." Your spurious experience isn't surprising, because you believe that being a Christian is "a mindset, a philosophy, a way of living." That's not the definition of a Christian. I had those things in my surfing days. Rather, a Christian is someone who knows the Lord (see John 17:3).

A false convert doesn't know Him (see 1 John 2:3-4; 1 John 4:6-8). He fakes it, but time exposes his hypocrisy. Judas is a good example of a false convert. He faked it for three and a half years. He was so trusted he looked after the finances, but the Bible says that he was a thief (see John 12:6). When Jesus said that one of the disciples would betray Him, they said, "Is it I, Lord?" They suspected themselves rather than the trusted treasurer. When Judas went out to betray Jesus, some of the disciples thought that he went to give money to the poor. He fooled everyone but God. The Scriptures tell us that Jesus knew from the beginning who would betray Him (see John 6:70).

Judas had no idea who Jesus was, even though he ate and drank with Him (as does the false convert, in taking communion). Judas didn't see Him as the ultimate treasure in an earthen vessel—God manifest in the flesh. When a woman broke an alabaster box of precious ointment and poured it on His feet as an act of worship, Judas complained that the money should have instead been given to the poor. Jesus wasn't worth it. He was only worth about thirty pieces of silver.

If you respond to me by saying that you were a genuine Christian, then you are admitting that you knew the Lord, that Jesus rose from the dead, and Christianity is therefore true. If you didn't know the Lord, then you were a false convert. You were either one or the other.

The other thought is, if you were of the disposition that you could be deceived, how do you know that it's not happening again? The essence of "deception" is that the deceived person doesn't know he's deceived. That is why we need God's Word as a guide.

If I had been through your experience, I would be as upset as you. Remember that Judas ended up hanging himself. So, be careful when you dine with atheists, because the sweet dishes they serve up contain undetected poison that will find its way into your very heart. They will feed you tasty Bible verses out of context, misquotes, and half-truths. The devil will give you enough rope to hang yourself. I would hate that to happen to you.

I'm just curious; am I correct in assuming that Ray and other Christians here all believe that Catholics, Methodists, Lutherans, Episcopal, and various other sects of Christianity are all false Christians, UNLESS they are born-again, and become Evangelical Fundamentalists?

The Bible doesn't mention "Catholics, Methodists, Lutherans, Episcopal," etc., instead, the Scriptures simply have two categories—the "just" and the "unjust." The "just" are those whom God has justified (made right with Himself through faith in Jesus). The "unjust" are those who are still in their sins. The Bible warns that God will see to it that every wicked person gets exactly what they have coming: "So it will be at the end of the age. The angels will come forth, separate the wicked from among the just, and cast them into the furnace of fire. There will be wailing and gnashing of teeth" (Matthew 13:49-50). That's good news for those who care about justice.

So, the question is, how is a person "justified"? This is what Martin Luther (a Catholic monk) asked hundreds of years ago. He found, through reading the Bible, that we are freely justified by God's mercy. The criminal is guilty, but the judge pays his fine. That's mercy. In Christ, God acquits us from the courtroom because Jesus paid our fine. Everlasting life is a free gift of God (see Romans 6:23). No one has to be "religious" to try to earn salvation from death. So who are the true Christians? Here is that answer from the Bible: "Nevertheless the solid foundation of God stands, having this seal: 'The Lord knows those who are His,' and, 'Let everyone who names the name of Christ depart from iniquity'" (2 Timothy 2:19). So make sure you are the Lord's, and that if you name the name of Christ, you depart from iniquity (violation of God's Law).

I agree with the famous words of Mahatma Gandhi, when he said, "I like your Christ, I do not like your Christians. Your Christians are so unlike your Christ."

First, no one is like Jesus Christ. He was sinless. If you think you can be like Him, try living like Him for one day. For one day fulfill the moral Law by loving God with all of your heart, mind, soul, and strength, and love your neighbor as much as you love yourself. That means you will not lust, hate, lie, steal, think a selfish thought, or say an idle word. You will be perfect, in thought, word, and deed. On top of that, you will walk in perfect humility of heart. If you think Gandhi did that, read on.

Second, the Bible doesn't tell us to place our trust in sinful man. In fact, it says not to (see Psalm 146:3). It instead commands that we repent and trust alone in Jesus Christ. This was something it seems Gandhi failed to do. So his liking of Jesus wasn't deep enough for him to believe what He said. Jesus warned that if we die in our sins, we will end up in hell. What a tragedy that Gandhi didn't find any help in his own hopeless religion. He lamented, "For it an unbroken torture to me that I am still so far from Him, Who as I fully know, governs every breath of my life, and Whose offspring I am. I know that it is the evil passions within that keep me so far from Him, and yet I cannot get away from them."[3]

Welcome to a dangerous new era—the Unlightenment—in which centuries of rational thought are overturned by idiots. Superstitious idiots. They're everywhere—reading horoscopes, buying homeopathic remedies, consulting psychics, babbling about "chakras" and "healing energies," praying to imaginary gods, and rejecting science in favor of soft-headed bunkum. But instead of slapping these people round the face till they behave like adults, we encourage them. We've got to respect their beliefs, apparently...Why should your outmoded codswallop be treated with anything other than the contemptuous mockery it deserves?

Mr. Atheist, I found myself saying a hearty "Amen" to everything you said. We *are* surrounded by weirdoes and crazies...superstitious simple-minded people who believe anything they are told. If the folks that write horoscopes really knew the future, they would all play blackjack, be super rich, and live in big mansions in Las Vegas and Reno, or they would have high-paying jobs on primetime TV, telling us about tomorrow's weather. My TV co-host and I snuck into a psychic store in Hollywood with a hidden camera and tried to expose them. We got kicked out, because our questions cut too close to the bone. Yep, amen to all the "healing" energy stuff and the "soft-headed bunkum," and another amen to the "imaginary gods" (a big amen to your small "g"). Man is forever making up false gods and bowing down to their images. It's crazy. Pizzas that look like Mary really turn my stomach. It is all "outmoded codswallop." Right on. You're not alone. Keep preaching it. We just go one step further and say to stop all this nonsense and to love and serve the Living God. I do make one small prediction, though (nothing psychic about me). My prediction is that this blog will make you mad. Then after you read that I said it will make you mad, you will decide that it won't. Then you will be a little confused as to how to respond. Let's see if I'm right.

What really shocks me here is the number of Christians who are afraid of atheists…What is scary about someone not believing the same thing as you…? Perhaps I am asking the wrong question… Perhaps I should be asking: are you that afraid that your belief system is that easily deconstructed…?

Good question. We are not scared of atheists, although if we weren't Christians, we should be. A very wise man once said, "Most I fear God. Next, I fear him who fears Him not." Atheists are probably about as dangerous as "religious" people (as opposed to those who truly love God). Religious people have killed millions throughout history in religious wars (the Crusades of the Catholic church, Islamic terrorism, etc.), the Spanish Inquisition (the murder of Christians by the Catholic church), the killing of the prophets of God (by religious Jews), the murder of Jesus, the persecution of the Church (see the Book of Acts for details, or read *Foxe's Book of Martyrs* for greater and horrific detail). Religious hypocrites come in a close second to atheistic communism, which is responsible for 100 million deaths throughout history. If someone doesn't fear God, they will lie to you (if they think that they can get away with it), they will steal from you (if they think they can get away with it), and they may even kill you (if they…you know why by now). The atheist thinks that he's getting away with his sin. He denies that there is a God, and therefore he believes that there is no judgment for his actions. He may evade civil law, but there is no way he can ever evade God's Law. God considers lust to be adultery, and hatred, murder. He sees the thought life, and Jesus warned that even every idle word he speaks, he will have to give an account for on the Day of Judgment.

I believe you were referring to me when you said an atheist asked if you talk to God. If this is the case, what I wanted to know was whether God talks back to you? You know, like a conversation. I ask in all sincerity.

No, God doesn't speak to me conversationally. Rather, I get direction through the Bible. We speak to God through prayer, and He speaks to us through His Word. The Scriptures are called a "lamp to our feet, and a light to our path." Couple that with the fact that the Holy Spirit leads us into all truth, and we are not left in the dark as is the rest of the world. We know our origins, the reason for our existence, and what's going to happen in the future.

Be very wary of people who hear voices in their heads, and say that God is speaking to them. The world is full of mentally unstable people (what are often called "religious nuts") who should be in an institution, but they are not (some would count me as one of them).

Then again, there are many sincere Christians who continually say things like, "God told me…" I'm sure that they take their cue from the television preachers who do the same thing. This brings great discredit to Christianity when it's found that "God" made a mistake (what He apparently told them doesn't come to pass). Having said all this, there are Christians who do believe that God speaks to us in a "small, still voice," and there are Scriptures that justify this. However, in the Old Testament, if a prophet said, "Thus says the Lord" and his prophecy didn't come to pass, he was deemed a false prophet and stoned to death. The key to judging whether something is from God is to ask, "Does it line up with God's Word?"

I once heard an elderly lady say, "I was going to leave my house and the Lord said, 'You're not going out until you wash your windows!'" I questioned her as to whether God did actually say that to her, and, of course, found that it was merely the voice of her conscience telling her that she should clean her filthy windows. I said, "Why then do you talk like that? It understandably makes Christians sound crazy."

Always remember that the Church is filled with false converts, something the Bible calls "tares" among the wheat, "bad fish" among the good, "foolish virgins" among the wise, etc. God will sort out the "sheep from the goats" on Judgment Day. However, in the meanwhile, they are the ones who the news media jump to for a hot story. It's big news when Mr. Wayne Bert says that he's the Messiah, and that God told him to get naked with young girls.

So don't take all these crazy things as a reason to reject Christianity. Jesus warned that many would come in His name saying that they were the "Christ"—the anointed One, the Messiah—and it sure is true. Mental homes are full of people who think that they are Jesus Christ. That's just another sign of His coming. Make sure you are ready.

God concept is not new to me. I've thought about it for years...many of us prayed when we were believers and got no response.

There is a difference between being a "believer" and being a Christian. Every sane human being is a "believer" in God's existence. Some people pretend He doesn't exist (atheists) but they know He does. I know what the atheist knows because God's Word tells me that He has given light to every man. He cannot plead ignorance.

Many a "believer" has prayed to God and "got no response" because he hasn't done what he has been commanded to do so that he will be heard. What would you think of me if I said that I didn't believe in cell phones because I tried using one and there was no response from the other person? I failed to turn the phone on and dial the number. That's the reason there was no response. You have to follow procedure to get a response from the other end of a phone and the same applies with calling on God.

The procedure for getting a response from God is to repent and then trust in Jesus Christ. Since I did that many years ago, I get a response every time I pray. Sometimes it's "Yes" from God. Sometimes there's a "No." Sometimes there's a "Please hold." This isn't in an audible voice, but through a certain conviction (like the voice of the conscience), through providential circumstances, or through His Word, the Bible.

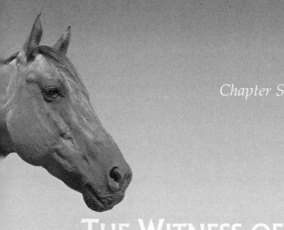

Chapter Seven

THE WITNESS OF JESUS CHRIST AND OF GOD'S HOLY SPIRIT

*"The Spirit Himself bears witness with our spirit
that we are children of God."*

—ROMANS 8:16

I *was in a New York synagogue*, wearing a spy camera. I must have stood out like a small white goose among a group of black penguins. These were orthodox Jews, and because I am Jewish, they let me attend the service. But I wasn't wearing black clothes or a black hat like the rest of them. I was in shorts and had special sunglasses sitting on my forehead.

Still, when they found that I had an uncle named Cohen, they treated me like royalty.

After the hour-long service, I made the mistake of handing a million dollar bill tract to a teenage boy. Suddenly the elders swooped on me and demanded, "Is this about JC?" They wouldn't even say the name of Jesus Christ. Within seconds, I (and my film crew who had joined me after the service) was on the sidewalk. I was guilty of the terrible crime of belonging to Jesus Christ, and their justice was swift for such wickedness.

The incident reminded me of a man who once approached me and cynically asked, "How's JC treating you?" I responded with, "Who is JC?" He smiled and said, "The Man upstairs." I replied, "Who?" He said, "The Big Three...Number One." I firmly asked, "What's His name?" He looked embarrassed, and walked off without saying a word.

Isn't it strange that sinners have such trouble saying His name in truth, but when they use it in blasphemy, it rolls off their tongue without a problem? It makes sense, though, that God's greatest act of love would ilicit the strongest reaction from sinners. They are still living in sin, still fighting the Holy Spirit, and therefore any reverential mention of Christ's sacrifice makes them uncomfortable. What He did on the Cross makes no sense to them. They don't believe Jesus was Who He said He was. Their very discomfort proves that the Spirit of God is real and active; otherwise, why would they feel anything at all at the mention of God or the name of Jesus Christ? Their discomfort is the Spirit's testimony to His existence and His desire for them to know Christ.

I do think that Jesus was a real man, but not the Son of God. Jesus had all the classic symptoms of schizophrenia. He often wandered off for days at a time; when he came back, he would go on and on about these very detailed and elaborate stories of being spoken to; he heard voices in his head...

It seems that you don't know who Jesus of Nazareth is or what He said. Perhaps you have sat through dry religious services, and have a mere perception of what He said. Schizophrenia is a psychiatric diagnosis that describes a mental illness characterized by "...disorganized speech and thinking in the context of significant social or occupational dysfunction."[1] Jesus is without question the most eloquent Man who ever lived. Those who heard Him said, "Never a man spoke like this Man." The most eloquent of philosophers sits at His feet and marvels at both His words and His life. To those who disagree, I would simply challenge you to read the Gospel of John, and see for yourself. Never did any man speak like this Man.

The Apostle Paul met this same Jesus, and it was the meeting on the Road to Damascus that turned him around from the road to damnation. Before that encounter, Paul was so anti-Christian he makes the ACLU look like choir boys. He breathed out hatred towards, persecuted, tortured, and murdered any believer in Jesus Christ into whom he could get his teeth.

You may claim that he merely saw a vision of Jesus. Not so. He met the Lord and came to "know Him, and the power of His resurrection."

He met Jesus and from that moment he was never the same. Meeting a celebrity can be a buzz. Meeting a president can be an honor. Meeting a king can be an amazing experience. But he or she who meets Jesus Christ and finds peace with God through His shed blood, finds everlasting life.

He had the disciples take the donkey without first asking the owner's permission. The owner agreed to it in the story, but still; try something like that in real life. Unless you've got a pre-arranged deal with someone, to just up and take something of theirs without asking permission first is the textbook definition of stealing.

Take a close look at Jesus Christ and see if you can find any sin in Him. You won't. He was morally perfect. The above is about the best anyone can do, along with He disobeyed His parents, or He lost His temper when He cleared the temple.

Let's deal with those three. The donkey. We have two accounts, one in Mark 11:1-6 and the other in Luke 19:29-35. Jesus told His disciples to go and get the donkey, and as they were untying him someone asked what they were doing, and they said what Jesus told them to say: "The Lord has need of him." Here's what any skeptic will find hard to swallow. The Lord Jesus Christ owned that donkey. He created every hair on its little head (see John 1:3 and Colossians 1:16), and you can't steal what you own. The temporal "owner" was in reality just taking care of it for Him.

How incredible to think that the Lord had need of a little donkey. But He did. He chose to be carried into Jerusalem on a lowly donkey. God has also chosen lowly creatures like us to carry the Savior to this sinful world. How incredible.

Number two problem—His "disobedience." In Luke 2:42-49 we are told that His mother and Joseph left Jerusalem "supposing Him to have been in the company." He wasn't. It took three days for them to find Him (thank God for cell phones). He was in the temple teaching the elders, as He said, about His "Father's business." Any responsible parent would never leave a city "supposing" that their twelve-year-old was with them. That was bad parenting by Mary and Joseph, not disobedience by Jesus.

Multitudes sit in churches "supposing" that Jesus is with them, but they don't know Him (see Matthew 7:21-23). They are false converts who will be sorted out on Judgment Day. They have never obeyed the command to repent and trust that Savior. That's disobedience.

Number three problem—Jesus lost His temper when He cleared the temple. The incident is recorded in all four Gospels. Here it is from John 2:14-16:

> And found in the temple those that sold oxen and sheep and doves, and the changers of money sitting. And when he had made a scourge of small cords, he drove them all out of the temple, and the sheep, and the oxen; and poured out the changers' money, and overthrew the tables; and said to them that sold doves, Take these things hence; make not my Father's house a house of merchandise.

The other three accounts give us a fuller picture. He also said, "It is written, My house shall be called the house of prayer; but you have made it a den of thieves."

There is no loss of temper here. What He did was deliberate and premeditated. He took the time to make a whip of small cords, then He cleared the temple of the money-hungry televangelists of His day. That should make any skeptic jump for joy. It does me.

There is another temple that should be a house of prayer, but is instead a den of thieves. God created us to be temples of His Holy Spirit, but we are instead inhabited by him who came to kill, steal, and destroy. Mr. Skeptic, let the ten cords of the whip of God's Law drive sin from your own money-hungry heart, and become a man of prayer instead of a finger-pointing skeptic.

I dare you. Study Jesus of Nazareth up close and personal. He is squeaky clean. He is morally perfect. I would never say that about any other human being, because there has never been one like Him.

Jesus was God manifest in the flesh: "And without controversy great is the mystery of godliness: God was manifest in the flesh, justified in the Spirit, seen of angels, preached unto the Gentiles, believed on in the world, received up into glory" (1 Timothy 3:16).

THE NATURE OF GOD HIMSELF

Mr. Comfort, I'm sure you've been asked this many times, but humor me: Could God create a boulder so heavy that he himself could not lift?

There are many things God cannot do. These are things related to His character rather than His ability. The Bible makes it clear that God cannot lie. It calls upon the strength of the word "impossible" to substantiate that He is trustworthy: "It is impossible for God to lie" (Hebrews 8:16). He cannot sin. All of His judgments are righteous and true altogether.

He also cannot let injustice go unpunished. If a man murders or rapes a woman, lies, steals, or commits adultery, he "stores up" God's wrath that will be revealed on Judgment Day.

In answer to the ancient question about the ability of God to create a rock that He cannot lift, I would answer that when it comes to the ability of God, nothing is impossible. Jesus did, however, speak of a large rock. He put it this way: "Whoever falls on that stone will be broken; but on whomever it falls, it will grind him to powder" (Luke 20:18). This was the same Jesus who said to love your enemies and to do good to those who spitefully use you. It was a strange thing for such a kind and loving person to say, until you understand what He said.

When you grind something to powder you do a thorough job. Nothing is left. That's how God's justice will be on Judgment day. He will not only punish murderers, but His just wrath will fall on those who have hated someone. He will not only punish adulterers and fornicators, but His just wrath will also fall on all those who have lusted after another person, lied, stolen, hated, blasphemed, etc. That's perfect and thorough justice. No sin (injustice) will be left unpunished.

Rather than being ground to powder by God's wrath, there is an alternative. Jesus said, "Whoever falls on that stone will be broken..." If you humble yourself and seek God's forgiveness (which is in Jesus Christ alone), you will have mercy. Otherwise the stone will fall upon you, which is very fearful.

So I hope I have more than humored you by reminding you that there is a massive stone of wrath abiding on you (see John 3:36), and that God has the ability to lift it off you, because of the Cross. It was on that Cross that Jesus took your punishment upon Himself, so that Eternal Justice wouldn't have to fall upon you.

Care to clarify: "nothing is impossible for God," so He can create a rock too large He cannot lift...If He can only do one, He is not infinite.

This question reveals a lack of common sense. The questioner thinks that if God couldn't create a rock too big for Him to lift then He doesn't exist. Then again, we could ask if God could make a perfectly round peg and put it into a perfectly square hole, and make it fit perfectly. Or, could God make an egg that's not an egg?

These are questions that are asked to divert attention away from the real issue. But it seems that God had the atheist pegged thousands of years ago when He said, "Do not answer a fool according to his folly, lest you also be like him."

One more of those dumb-sounding questions, that may not be dumb. Could God take a man who is a fool but thinks that he's wise, and make him see that he is a fool, so that he will be wise? The answer is in 1 Corinthians 3:18.

The God that I read about in the Bible is quite capricious. You never know when he might smite one.

I can understand why you feel that the God of the Bible is capricious. To you, His judgments make no sense. They are irrational. That's because you are not God. I'm not being facetious. I reminding you that you aren't omniscient. It is because He has all knowledge that all of His judgments are righteous and true altogether. Your knowledge is extremely limited, so how could you begin to understand the judgments of Almighty God?

Let's look at your moral judgments for a moment. Do you think homosexuality is morally wrong? Of course you don't (I'm guessing). How about fornication? Adultery? Murder? Rape? Lying and stealing? If you say that any of these things are morally wrong, from where do you get your standard of judgment? Is it your own moral standard? Perhaps you say that it's whatever society considered to be morally correct. So then if society says that homosexuality is morally okay, then you agree. If society says that fornication (sex outside of marriage) is okay, then you agree. Then if society says that it's morally right to exterminate Jews, then you must say that it's okay, because you have no moral absolutes.

The thought of you ending up in hell grieves me. I can hardly entertain it. But I know that if a holy and perfect God judges you by His perfect moral standard, that is where you will end up. You may go kicking and screaming (like a murderer to the electric chair), but you will still go there. Please look for a moment at the Ten Commandments. Go through them and ask yourself if you have kept them in the light of what Jesus said in the Sermon on the Mount. If you are honest, you will have to come to the same conclusion that I came to one night in 1972. I am a sinner. I need a Savior.

God sent a flood to kill everybody except for Noah and his family because the world was full of evil. God knows everything. The world is still full of evil after the flood and God, by definition, must have known that would be the case: but He killed everybody anyway, including children, babies, and pregnant women. How can you justify this?

The difference between the godly and ungodly is that the godly (those who have been regenerated by the Holy Spirit) will always justify God. The ungodly will try to justify man.

So let's demonstrate the truth of the above statement. I am convinced from Scripture and from experience that mankind (there's an oxymoron) is intrinsically evil. For evidence, just watch the TV news tonight. He is born with a sinful nature and goes astray from the moment he takes his first step (no parent has to restrain a child from being virtuous, but rather the opposite). Children instinctively know how to be selfish, to lie, to be rebellious, etc. We have to *teach* them to share, to speak the truth, and to be obedient.

God, however, is perfect. He is without sin. He is absolute purity of holiness. He cannot have an evil thought or make an evil decision. The Bible tells us that all of His judgments are righteous and true altogether.

Let me now presume that you will attempt to justify man, by saying that he is basically good, and that God is the One who is evil. (I did notice that you said "the world is full of evil," rather than man is full of evil—which would include yourself.) You therefore choose not to worship and serve a God that you consider to be a tyrant. That's your choice, but know for certain that you will one day meet your "tyrant" Maker, stand before His absolute holiness, and be judged for the sins you have committed. If you refuse the incredible mercy that He offers in Christ, then you will be justly damned in hell for eternity.

God, however, will not condemn you. Your sins will do that, in the same way that it's not the judge who sends the wicked criminal to prison. His crimes send him there.

As Thomas Paine put it, rather more concisely, this was "an order to butcher the boys, to massacre the mothers and debauch the daughters." There are many occasions of the Lord waxing wrath against the people of Israel, never mind the numerous tribes that they came into conflict with who were massacred or enslaved. The oddest example that springs to mind is in Exodus 32…Which suggests that the Lord committed an evil act in contemplating wrath of which he only repented when Moses promised to conquer the lands on his behalf. How could he repent unless he had done something wrong in the first place?

If you think that's bad, how about the fact that God has proclaimed the death sentence upon every man, woman, and child? It gets worse. Eternal damnation in a terrible place called hell awaits everyone who has done evil. Everyone. The day will come when absolute justice will be done. That's wonderful news…if you are not a criminal in God's eyes. And if His judgments upset you, here's a verse for you to think about: "All of

God's judgments are righteous and true altogether." I trust Him and I am not at all offended by anything He does. You don't, and you are offended. There's a reason for that. Let's now talk about your sins for a moment. Have you ever lusted after a woman? Have you lied or stolen or used God's name in vain? If you are like the rest of us and have done those things, you are a lying, thieving, blasphemous, adulterer at heart (see Matthew 5:27-28). Then who are you to stand in moral judgment over Almighty God! Delusions of grandeur, indeed. Humble yourself and you will see things as they are.

What we are dealing with is a petty tyrant and self-proclaimed authority. I certainly have no reason to believe he has my best interest at heart (or mankind's best interest, for that matter). He seems a terrible despot who would inflict suffering because he enjoyed hearing the screams.

You feel like that because you don't see your own sins as they are. Your attitude is the same as that of an unrepentant criminal has toward a good judge. He thinks his judgments against his rape and murder are "petty," and in doing so reveals his attitude toward his own crimes. He thinks his crimes are inconsequential. He believes that the reason the judge sends him to prison is simply because he wants him to suffer, because he enjoys it.

Rather, the judge sends him to prison to carry out justice—to do that which is right, just, and good. If he is a good judge, he gets no pleasure in seeing another person suffer, but he will resolutely see that the sentence is carried out. He, no doubt, would rather see a criminal broken and sorrowful for his heinous crimes, than proud, self-righteous, and unrepentant.

And God is the same. The Bible says that He takes no pleasure in the death of the wicked. His Word even says that mercy "rejoices over judgment," meaning that God would rather see someone sorrowful and repentant and have their sins forgiven, than receive the full wrath of His justice.

But if they remain hard and impenitent, check out what His Word warns:

113

> But in accordance with your hardness and your impenitent heart you are treasuring up for yourself wrath in the day of wrath and revelation of the righteous judgment of God, who *"will render to each one according to his deeds"*: eternal life to those who by patient continuance in doing good seek for glory, honor, and immortality; but to those who are self-seeking and do not obey the truth, but obey unrighteousness—indignation and wrath, tribulation and anguish, on every soul of man who does evil, of the Jew first and also of the Greek; but glory, honor, and peace to everyone who works what is good, to the Jew first and also to the Greek. For there is no partiality with God (Romans 2:5-11).

You just don't get it, Ray. Your God is so psychotic that I wouldn't worship Him even if you could prove He was real, which thank God, you can't. Your own Holy Book says that your God drowned 99.9999 percent of all air-breathing life on the planet. Kittens, Ray. He drowned jillions of kittens—and you worship Him. Are you crazy or what? Captain H.

Why are you so upset? As an atheist, you believe that no one made the kittens. There was nothing, and then, over time, there were jillions of cute kittens. Besides, for an atheist, life has no rhyme nor reason, and there's no absolute right and there's no absolute wrong. So, in your book, God ultimately didn't do anything morally wrong.

Are you as angry at veterinarians (who in the United States kill around 12 million cats each year) as you are at God? They kill them, Captain. Cats and kittens (and dogs). When did you last get angry enough about cat and kitten deaths to picket outside a vet clinic?

Besides, if God made the kittens, He has the right to kill them, if He sees fit to do so. I'm sure you know that cats breed like rabbits. Can you imagine how overrun the earth would be by now if God hadn't killed those jillions of kittens?

So, the next time you are upset about God and His judgments, remember that if cats came by the process of evolution (and all cats die), God didn't kill them, evolution did. So get mad at your own beliefs and lighten up when it comes to others. Live and let live.

Didn't God make the homosexuals gay to begin with? Are they not also in his image? What sort of sick God would make gay people, and then send them to hell if they didn't repent and become heterosexuals? Is this another bizarre test of morality?

Some time ago I viewed one of our upcoming TV programs called "Joe Average." It looks closely at an average Joe who doesn't

---

Atheists Evolved from Chickens

A loving Christian brother just emailed me and said, "Man, oh, man. There are some bitter, furious, Christian hatin' bloggers out there!!!" I told him that he is seeing comparatively nice ones. They know that I delete anything with blasphemy or cussing. He's right though. Some of the atheists that are part of this blog are pretty nasty. So, I have decided to return a bit of the fire (in love, of course).

My new theory is that perhaps atheists evolved from the chicken, because they not only have chicken characteristics—a head, eyes, mouth, skin, neck, heart, earlobes and legs (homology structures), but they also have the chicken's tendencies—they are chicken-livered. They hang around Christians like annoying little bugs hang around light, trying to inject their poison whenever they can.

If you are an atheist, I hope I'm ruffling your feathers. I want to get under your skin and ask why you don't have the courage to even whisper to Muslims what you keep shouting at Christians. Prove me wrong. Get onto a Muslim Web site and tell them that you don't believe their god exists. Do your little "I don't believe in Zeus" thing. Tell them they believe a myth. Make sure you use the word "fairytale." Talk about Mohammed as you do Jesus (use your usual lower case for Mohammed). Do your "I don't believe in the flying spaghetti monster" thing. Tell them that you believe that they weren't made by (a) god, but that they evolved from primates (that will go down well).

Explain that you think they are blind simpletons to believe the way they do, and that even though there is a creation, you don't see any evidence that there is a Creator. Let them know that you think that it's intelligent to believe the way you do. You may as well explain that even though you don't believe in God's existence, you use His name as a cuss word, because you think it's worthless. Also, let them know in no uncertain terms that you believe that the Koran is full of mistakes (give some examples), and that their mosques are full of hypocrites.

You wouldn't dare, because you are chicken-livered. You know that they are not like Christians. Despite the "anonymity" of your little chicken coop, they would come after you to lop off your head. And when they find you, you would fall on your knees and be praying to God for help, quicker than I can move a fly swatter...and I'm pretty quick. So, think about what you are doing, and think about how much you value your life. Then think about what we are telling you. Think.

---

think much about creation, let alone his Creator. If you asked Joe if God had ever done anything for him, he probably couldn't think of a thing. Then the program looks at what a miracle not only Joe is, but the absolute of everything around him—from the honey on his toast, to the milk in his early morning drink.

The program is amazing. It glorifies God in a wonderfully unique way and had us "wowing" at what our production and graphics department had managed to do.

Some time later I was watching a program about sea life in Indonesia. To say that the underwater life was amazing is a gross understatement. It was breathtaking. It made me think about the Creator and how pathetic our TV program was in its attempt to reveal His glory. It made me think how pathetic I am in trying to relate to a godless world how magnificent God is, and how pathetic we are as we gather in church to sing praise to Him. Yet, the irony is that God is glorified in our pathetic attempts to glorify Him. He has condescended to use humanity to reach humanity, and He has "chosen the foolishness of preaching to save them that believe."

"His consequent rising from the dead means that God can now legally commute our death sentence." That suggests that God is under some law. Whose law? If God is Jesus and Jesus is God, why did Jesus have to have himself killed to forgive us, that is, why does our "debt have to be paid"?

God is more than "under some law." He cannot be separated from the moral Law. The Bible says that God is "perfect, holy, just, and good." It also says that His Law is "perfect, holy, just, and good." In other words the moral Law (the Ten Commandments) issue from the very character and nature of God. There wasn't a time in eternity when He asked, "What is right and what is wrong?" The moral Law is eternal. That's why Jesus said that heaven and earth would pass away before one "jot" or "tittle" of the Law would fail. It is written in stone. It's not going away and it's not going to change. It is immutable, and it calls for the blood of every guilty criminal.

Think of it like this. A man has viciously raped and murdered six young girls. There is no question of his guilt. He is not insane. He said he enjoyed what he did, and if he had opportunity, he would do it again. As the good judge looks at the evidence of his knife, the man's fingerprints all over it, his DNA, his letter of confession, and the photos of the young mutilated girls with their throats cut, how he is going to feel? Is he going to be passive? Of course not. As he looks at the smiling criminal, the judge's wrath will be in direct proportion to his goodness. If he is a good judge, he will be unspeakably furious at that wicked man. He will throw the book at him and sentence him to the maximum punishment under the law.

God's wrath is in direct proportion to His perfect goodness. There is no question of our guilt. All of us have violated His Law. We are filled with lust, greed, selfishness, ingratitude, lies, hate, envy, jealousy, conceit, etc., and His just wrath therefore abides on us (see John 3:36). If we are found in our sins on Judgment Day, He will throw the Book at us, and hell will be exactly what we deserve.

But the Bible says that this holy God is rich in mercy, and He provided a way for us to escape the wrath of His Law. You asked, "If God is Jesus and Jesus is God, why did Jesus have to have himself killed to forgive us, that is, why does our 'debt have to be paid'?" Actually, contrary to popular thought, Jesus didn't have to "die" for our sins. Obviously, He did die, but the Bible says that He had to "suffer" for our sins (see Luke 24:26; 1 Peter 3:18). This is made clear in the fact that the debt was paid before he died—He cried, "It is finished," then He died.

The Judge Himself came down to the courtroom, and paid the fine in His life's blood. That demonstrates both the justice of a holy God, and the love of a merciful God. Those two attributes of the Divine nature are revealed in the Cross, and you will never understand that until you humble your heart.

I once stopped a couple on rollerblades and asked if they would like to be on television, talking about what they believe happens after someone dies. They looked at each other and said, "We're atheists!" I told them how much I love atheists, and they gave their consent to be on the program.

First question: "Has God ever done anything for you?" Their answer was a predictable "Nothing." I said, "He gave you life." Again, a predictable "Our parents gave us life." I said, "That's right. And their parents gave them life, right back to Adam." He agreed, then said, "No!!!!" He laughed, and added "You got me!" That set a relaxed tone for the interview.

I said, "I have a task for you. Make me some milk, from nothing."

He looked a bit puzzled and said, "We would need a cow."

"Okay then, make me a cow, from nothing." He said he couldn't do it. His wife agreed. So I asked where the first cow came from.

"Evolution."

"How did evolution create the cow?"

A predictable, "The big bang."

"Where did the materials come from for the big bang to happen?"

He didn't know.

When I asked them both to make me some honey, from nothing, they went back to the bee, and ended up with the same dilemma. They had no idea what happened "in the beginning."

I asked them to surmise that there was a God in the beginning, and a heaven and a hell. Were they good enough to go to heaven? A predictable, of course they were…that is, until they saw the perfect righteousness of God's Law—they were guilty of lying, stealing, blasphemy, and adultery of the heart (lust). If there was a hell, they both admitted that they were going there when they died. Did that concern them? It did. I then explained that two thousand years ago a legal transaction took place between God and man.

When Jesus of Nazareth suffered and died on the Cross, He was paying the fine for the moral Law that each of us has transgressed. Because of His suffering, death, and resurrection, God can now legally dismiss our case. We can leave the courtroom. He can commute our death sentence and let us live.

I explained the necessity of repentance and faith, and how (if the husband cared about his wife and five kids) he needed to get right with God. He looked at me with wide eyes and said, "I have never had anyone explain that to me before…" It was a wonderful interview with a couple of very nice people. It was also just what we needed for the program. It wasn't the first time atheists turned out to be a Godsend.

CONCLUSION

Imagine I offered you a choice of four gifts:

- The original *Mona Lisa*
- The keys to a brand new Lamborghini
- Ten million dollars in cash
- A parachute

You can pick only one. Which would you choose? Before you decide, here's some information that will help you to make the wisest choice: *You have to jump ten thousand feet out of an airplane.*

Does that help you to connect the dots? It should, because you *need* the parachute. It's the only one of the four gifts that will help with your dilemma. The others may have some value, but they are useless when it comes to facing the law of gravity in a ten thousand-foot fall. The knowledge that you will have to jump should produce a healthy fear in you—and that kind of fear is good because it can save your life. Remember that.

Now think of the four major religions:

- Hinduism
- Buddhism
- Islam
- Christianity

Which one should you choose? Before you decide, here's some information that will help you determine which one is the wisest choice: All of humanity stands on the edge of eternity. We are *all* going to die. We will all have to pass through the door of death. It could happen to us in twenty years, or in six months...or today.

For most of humanity, death is a huge and terrifying plummet into the unknown. So what should we do?

Do you remember how it was your knowledge of the law of gravity that produced that healthy fear, and that fear helped you to make the best choice? You know what the law of gravity can do to you at ten thousand feet. In the same way, your knowledge of the moral Law will hopefully help you make the best choice with life's greatest issue—what happens when you die.

The Bible tells us that when we take that "unknown" leap and pass through the door of death, we have to face "the law of sin and death"—the Ten Commandments. As we have seen, we are without excuse when we stand before God because He gave us our conscience to know right from wrong. Each time we lie, steal, commit adultery, and so on, we know that it is wrong.

As we have looked at this subject, you may have developed a sense of fear. Remember to let that fear work for your good. The fear of God is the healthiest fear you can have. The Bible calls it "the beginning of wisdom."[1]

Let's now look at those four major religions to see which one, if any, can help you with your predicament.

Hinduism: The religion of Hinduism says that if you've been bad, you may come back as a rat or some other animal.[2] If you've been good, you might come back as a prince. But that's like someone saying, "When you jump out of the plane, you'll get sucked back in as another passenger. If you've been bad, you go down to the Economy Class; if you've been good, you go up to First Class." It's an interesting concept, but it doesn't deal with your real problem of having sinned against God and the reality of hell. And there is no evidence for this belief.

Buddhism: Amazingly, the religion of Buddhism denies that God even exists. It says that life and death are sort of an illusion.[3] That's like standing at the door of the plane and saying, "I'm not really here, and there's no such thing as the law of gravity, and no ground that I'm going to hit." That may temporarily help you deal with your fears, but it doesn't square with reality. And it doesn't deal with your real problem of having sinned against God and the reality of hell.

Islam: Interestingly, Islam acknowledges the reality of sin and hell, and the justice of God, but the hope it offers is that sinners can escape God's justice if they do religious works. God will see these, *and because of them,* hopefully He will show mercy—but they won't know for sure.[4] Each person's works will be weighed on the Day of Judgment and it will then be decided who is saved and who is not—based on whether they followed Islam, were sincere in repentance, and performed enough righteous deeds to outweigh their bad ones.

So Islam believes you can earn God's mercy by your own efforts. But that's like jumping out of the plane, and believing that flapping your arms is going to counter the law of gravity and save you from a ten thousand-foot drop.

And there's something else to consider. The Law of God shows us that even the best of us is nothing more than a guilty criminal, standing guilty and without excuse before the throne of a perfect and holy Judge. When that is understood, then our "righteous deeds" are actually seen as an attempt to bribe the Judge of the Universe. The Bible says that because of our guilt, anything we offer God for our justification (to get ourselves off the hook) is an abomination to Him.[5] Islam, like the other religions, cannot save you from the consequences of sinning against God.

Christianity: So why is Christianity different? Aren't all religions the same? Let's see. In Christianity, God Himself provided a "parachute" for us, and the Bible says regarding the Savior, "Put on the Lord Jesus Christ."[6] Just as a parachute solved your dilemma with the law of gravity and its consequences, so the Savior perfectly solves your dilemma with the Law of God and its consequences! It is the missing puzzle-piece that you need.

How did God solve our dilemma? He satisfied His wrath by becoming a human being and taking our punishment upon Himself. The Scriptures tell us that God was in Christ, reconciling the world to Himself. Christianity provides the only parachute to save us from the consequences of the Law we have transgressed.

BACK TO THE PLANE

In looking at the four major religions to see if they can help us in our dilemma, we find that Christianity fits the bill perfectly. To illustrate this more clearly, let's go back to that plane for a moment. You are standing on the edge of a ten thousand-foot drop. You have to jump. Your heart is thumping in your chest. Why? Because you know that the law of gravity will kill you when you jump.

Someone offers you the original *Mona Lisa*. You push it aside. Another person passes you the keys to a brand new Lamborghini. You let them drop to the floor. Someone else tries to put ten million dollars into your hands. You push the hand away, and stand there in horror at your impending fate. Suddenly, you hear a voice say, "Here's a parachute!"

Which one of those four people is going to hold the most credibility in your eyes? It's the one who held up the parachute! Again, it is your knowledge of the law of gravity and your fear of the jump that turns you toward the good news of the parachute.

In the same way, knowledge of what God's moral Law will do to you on the Day of Judgment produces a fear that makes the Gospel unspeakably good news! It solves your predicament of God's wrath. God became a sinless human being in the person of Jesus of Nazareth. The Savior died an excruciating death on the Cross, taking your punishment (the death penalty) upon Himself, and the demands of eternal justice were satisfied the moment He cried, "It is finished!" The Bible tells us, "Christ has redeemed us from the curse of the law, having been made a curse for us."[7] We broke the Law, but God became a man to pay our penalty with His own life's blood.

Then He rose from the dead, defeating death. This means that God can forgive every sin you have ever committed and commute your death sentence. When you repent (turn from your sins) and place your faith in Jesus Christ, you can say with the apostle Paul: For the law of the Spirit of life in Christ Jesus has made me free from the law of sin and death.[8]

So you no longer need to be afraid of death, and you don't need to look any further for ways to make peace between you and God. The Savior is God's gift to you. It is unspeakably good news! Now God Himself can "justify" you. He can wash you clean and give you the "righteousness" of Christ. He can save you from death and hell, and grant you everlasting life—something that you could never earn or deserve.

So if you haven't yet repented and trusted the Savior, please do it now. Simply tell God you are sorry for your sins, then *turn* from them, and place your trust in Jesus Christ alone to save you. Don't wait until tomorrow. It may never come.

THE IMMIGRATION DEPARTMENT

Rick is my plumber. Each time we needed to have something fixed at the ministry or at my home, I grew to know him better and like him more. That's because Rick is a nice guy—a typical genuine Christian. He has a warm personality, and is friendly and hardworking.

One day Rick told me that he was taking his family to New Zealand for a vacation. I was thrilled. New Zealand is my home country, and it really is beautiful. He was flying seven thousand miles from Los Angeles to the city of Auckland and then driving to the Bay of Islands for some snorkeling and deep-sea fishing.

A short time later he was back. He explained that, while flying into Auckland, his wife filled out the necessary customs and immigration forms. Her eyes fell on one question on her husband's form. It asked, "Have you been arrested?" She hesitated. Rick had spent time in jail before he was a Christian. Then she answered yes.

An hour or so later, they arrived in Auckland and excitedly went through the entrance procedure. As he waited at customs, an officer looked at the checked box on the declaration card. He looked at Rick and said, "You will need to speak with immigration." Immigration then told him that they needed to ask him a few questions. It was nothing personal, but they had to write down everything he said. It was a very mechanical process. Why had he been arrested? It was for burglary, to support a drug habit. How long had he spent in jail? More than a year. Would he use drugs in New Zealand? Rick politely answered all of their questions, and even shared the Gospel with them. He had to, because they asked him how he was able to break his drug habit. They then left him for a short time, returned, and said that in 1978 New Zealand had passed a law prohibiting anyone who had been in jail for more than twelve months from entering New Zealand. They were very sorry, but it was not negotiable. He had to return to the United States.

Rick went back to his wife and kids and told them the bad news. They would have to go on without him. The family cried bitterly together, and then they reluctantly separated.

When I found out what had happened, I was both embarrassed and angry. How could my home country treat my friend so horribly! As a Christian, Rick was now a new person. What's more, he was honest enough to admit the truth about his past. I wanted to complain to someone, but I couldn't...because New Zealand had the right to set its own standards of entry. heaven has done the same. No lawbreaker will ever enter its gates. Not a soul. So if you want to avoid hell, it would be wise for you to check out the standard of entry into heaven, before you try to get in. Here it is:

> There shall by no means enter it anything that defiles, or causes an abomination or a lie, but only those who are written in the Lamb's Book of Life...But the cowardly, unbelieving, abominable, murderers, sexually immoral, sorcerers, idolaters, and all liars shall have their part in the lake which burns with fire and brimstone, which is the second death (Revelation 21:8, 21:27).

However, unlike with New Zealand, there is a way to have your criminal record permanently expunged—completely removed so you have a clean record. In addition to having your past washed away, you become a brand new person.

HE MADE A WAY

The Bible tells us that this same Judge who will find you guilty of breaking His Law is also rich in mercy. He has made a way for you to be forgiven. "For God so loved the world that He gave His only begotten Son, that whoever believes in Him should not perish but have everlasting life."[9]

If there was one chance in a million that this is true, you owe it to your good sense to consider it with an open heart. God offers everlasting life to all humanity, and promises, "Their sins and their lawless deeds I will remember no more" (Hebrews 10:17). What you must do in response is to "repent" (not simply confess your sins, but *turn* from them), and trust the Savior (not just a belief, but a "trust"—as you would trust a parachute to save you). The moment you do that, God reveals Himself to you—not in a vision or in a voice, but He does so by giving you His Holy Spirit to live inside you. He makes you brand new on the inside, so that you want to do that which is pleasing to Him.

That's a miracle for a sin-loving sinner like me. That happened to me on April 25, 1972, at 1:30 in the morning, and after all these years I am still shaking my head at the radical nature of my conversion. It's so radical that the Bible calls it being "born again." In one moment I was made a new person.

It's like this. If I look at a heater and *believe* the heater is hot, I have an intellectual belief. But if I say to myself, "I wonder if it really *is* hot" and reach out and grip the bar, the second my flesh burns, I stop *believing* it's hot, I now *know* it's hot. I have moved out of the realm of *belief* into the realm of *experience*.

That's what will happen to you the moment you are born again (when you become a Christian). You will move out of the realm of "belief" into the realm of "personal experience." A Christian is not someone who has a "belief," but someone who has a relationship with the living God. You come to *know* Him. You will say with the writer of "Amazing Grace," "I once was blind, but now I see."

SOME PERSONAL QUESTIONS

Do you like to snuggle up in a warm bed on a cold night? Do you have a favorite position for going to sleep? Have you ever woken from a nightmare, and taken about ten minutes to shake off a feeling of terror?

Has your whole body suddenly "jumped" because you thought you were taking a step, just before you dropped off to sleep?

Do you get annoyed when someone asks you personal questions, or do you feel a sense of identification because you have had these experiences?

I hope you do identify with me. The reason for this is that it's my knowledge that you are just like me that drives me to try to reach you with the Gospel.

Whether you like it or not, you *are* like me. You have many of the same loves, fears, desires, and concerns. You, like me, want to enjoy the pleasures of this life. No one in his right mind wants to be unhappy, and you therefore instinctively don't want to die. Everything within you pulls back from the experience of death. It's the ultimate root canal for which there is no painkiller outside of conversion to Jesus Christ.

So, if you don't know the Lord, ask yourself some personal questions about me. What is my motive for pleading with you like this? I don't get paid for having a blog. I don't sell advertising on it. I have never asked for your money, nor do I want it. Christianity doesn't do anything for my ego. Neither is my motive to get you to join a church or a religion. It's simply a deep concern for your eternal welfare. Please, repent and trust the Savior before death seizes on you, and it's too late.

THE ATHEIST STARTER KIT

If you are a beginner atheist, there's a belief system you should embrace and a language you should learn, or you will find yourself in trouble. Here are ten suggestions for the novice:

1. Whenever you are presented with credible evidence for God's existence, call it a "straw man argument," or "circular reasoning." If something is quoted from somewhere, label it "quote mining."

2. When a Christian says that creation proves that there is a Creator, dismiss such common sense by saying "That's just the old watchmaker argument."

3. When you hear that you have everything to gain and nothing to lose (the pleasures of heaven, and the endurance of hell) by obeying the Gospel, say "That's just the old 'Pascal wager.'"

4. You can also deal with the "whoever looks on a woman to lust for her, has committed adultery with her already in his heart," argument by saying that there is no evidence that Jesus existed. None.

5. Believe that the Bible is full of mistakes, and actually says things like the world is flat. Do not read it for yourself. That is a big mistake. Instead, read, believe, and imitate Richard Dawkins. Learn and practice the use of big words. "Megalo-maniacal, sadomasochistic, capriciously malevolent bully" is a good phrase to learn.

6. Say that you were once a genuine Christian, and that you found it to be false. (The cool thing about being an atheist is that you can lie through your teeth, because you believe that are no moral absolutes.) Additionally, if a Christian points out that this is impossible (simply due to the very definition of Christianity as one who knows the Lord), just reply "That's the 'no true Scotsman fallacy.'" PLEASE NOTE: It cannot be overly emphasized how learning and using these little phrases can help you feel secure in dismissing common sense.

7. Believe that nothing is 100 percent certain, except the theory of Darwinian evolution. Do not question it. Believe with all of your heart that there is credible scientific evidence for species-to-species transitional forms. When you make any argument, pat yourself on the back by concluding with "Man, are you busted!" That will make you feel good about yourself.

8. Deal with the threat of eternal punishment by saying that you don't believe in the existence of hell. Then convince yourself that because you don't believe in something, it therefore doesn't exist. Don't follow that logic onto a railway line and an oncoming train.

9. Blame Christianity for the atrocities of the Roman Catholic church—when it tortured Christians through the Spanish Inquisition, imprisoned Galileo for his beliefs, or when it murdered Muslims in the Crusades.

10. Finally, keep in fellowship with other like-minded atheists who believe as you believe, and encourage each other in your beliefs. Build up your faith. Never doubt for a moment. Remember, the key to atheism is to be unreasonable. Fall back on that when you feel threatened. Think shallow, and keep telling yourself that you are intelligent. Remember, an atheist is someone who pretends there is no God.

LUNCH WITH AN ATHEIST

The boss of a "backyard" atheistic skeptics club recently asked me to have lunch with him. Bruce was a nice man, so we made a date to eat together. After saying grace, we chatted for about forty minutes and then went back to our ministry to answer some questions his fellow skeptics had formulated. As we sat down, he boldly put a small recording device into my top pocket. I felt as though I was being set up, but decided to see where he was leading me.

They were the usual questions skeptics ask. Here are a few, from memory: "Why do you reject all the evidence of evolution given by paleontologists?" I told him that I was a skeptic by nature, and that evidence for evolution given by paleontologists should be viewed with great skepticism, because they had big motives for lying. If a paleontologist comes up with any sort of evidence, he could find his face on the cover of *National Geographic*, with worldwide TV interviews, a book deal, and big honorariums for speaking engagements. So, the modern paleontologist has a huge incentive for twisting the truth, just a little.

The next question was "Why doesn't God show Himself by doing a little miracle, like simply moving a glass of water on the desk in front us?" I told him that over lunch he mocked the miracle of God causing the sun to stand still for Joshua. That was bigger and better than the moving glass. Besides, if he wanted an audience with the Queen of England, she doesn't come on his terms, he comes on hers. He mumbled, "Good analogy."

He then asked me why there were so many religions. I told him that man messes up everything to which he puts his hand—especially religion, that I hate religion, and I explained that the difference between being a Christian and being "religious" is something called "works righteousness." Religious people think that they can earn (or bribe) their way to heaven by doing things—fasting, praying, facing Mecca, doing good works, etc., when eternal life is a free gift of God. It can't be earned. I said that I would rather be called "stumpy" than "religious." Religion has caused untold wars and misery throughout history, it's the opium of the masses, and I don't run around in a white robe sprinkling water on people.

He also brought up the "banana" argument. Years ago, I published a booklet called "The Atheist Test." In the booklet, I compare a banana to a coke can (with its own tab, etc.). It's a parody, using a little humor to make a point. "The Atheist Test" has proven to be very popular (over a million have sold). However, it wasn't too popular with atheists. They removed the coke can portion of the parody, maintained that I believe the banana is proof for God's existence, and sure made a monkey out of me.

As I was answering his questions, I was thinking that things weren't going the way my friend expected. I became convinced that he wouldn't post the interview on the skeptics' Web site. It wasn't good for his cause.

The next time I saw Bruce, my thoughts were confirmed. He said that he had decided not to post it because I had mentioned the Bible too many times. If I recall correctly, I may have referred to it two or three times. Besides, he was in the broadcasting business, but I guess he must have forgotten about something called "editing."

The incident confirmed what I had believed all along. The skeptic isn't interested in truth. He only wants to confirm his presuppositions. That's why they have their club—to build up each other in their faith (beliefs). How true that "Men love darkness rather than light; neither will they come to the light, least their deeds are exposed." Oops. I quoted the Bible.

LUNCH WITH A CHRISTIAN

I noticed that one or two cynically said that they would like to see the atheist's perspective of our lunch. So here it is:

"Had a good lunch today with Ray Comfort. Why, do you ask, would I consider spending an hour with an evangelical Christian preacher saving souls through open-air preaching? Isn't he the 'enemy'? Previously, we spoke to each other at the pier, and even though we have several major disagreements, we also exchanged some thoughts on what we do agree on. I thought it was a worthwhile venture—and it was.

"Ray generally thinks most atheists are like the ones he debates on national TV. Of course, those atheist debaters pull no punches and let Ray have it—and sometimes not in a nice, gentle way! I wanted to let him know that most unreligious people and atheists are just like him, you and me—trying to make a living and stay afloat while seeking their own truth about our natural world.

"Ray introduced me to his wife, his CFO, and all the other employees of his 'Living [Waters] Ministries' nonprofit center in Bellflower, CA. Even though I introduced myself as 'Bruce—the good atheist' everyone was friendly and even chuckled a bit at the obvious ironic intro (an atheist visiting an all-Jesus-loving, Bible-thumping ministry).

"Before lunch, Ray showed me his bicycle he rides to work every day. I learned he doesn't own a car, but borrows his wife's car when he needs to. He doesn't like faith healers (a common opinion with me) and doesn't like the Catholic Church's spending policies. In a short, recorded interview after lunch, he said he doesn't consider himself 'religious'—meaning he is trying to save souls through his ministry and doesn't belong to any [particular] Christian denomination. His ministry is a 501C3 nonprofit group and his income is listed for the public to see. He owns the same

$195,000 house that he purchased 19 [13] years ago. He flies coach everywhere he goes, and doesn't ask for any fee for speaking—only if the congregation takes a collection does he get paid. He does ask for one thousand in attendance due to some previously low-attended seminars he went to somewhere in Idaho, far from any airport or major city.

"Even though we are worlds apart theoretically, Ray impressed me with many humorous and sometimes corny jokes and gags around his office, was genuinely friendly, humble, and honest. I hope he learned from our lunch that all atheists are not like the ones on TV. I learned that all preachers on TV are not like the ones—well, on TV!

"This…proves that some ideas can be agreed upon—even with the widest separation of ideologies. Maybe it could be a lesson for other extreme thinkers."

IN COMPLETE CONTROL

Hello. My name is "Unreasonable." I am a very proud demon. I love to hate, and I live for lust. I am extremely prejudiced. Come too close, and I will hiss out my venom. I don't fear God or man, and I live in the House of Atheist.

If you want to enter my house, know that I control who and what gets in, and I'm in complete control of what comes out. Try knocking to see if I will open the door. Before you even try, let me tell you that I despise truth and will not let it enter…unless I think it's in my best interests.

Take the subject of bats. The Bible says that bats are "birds," probably because they have wings and fly. That's ridiculous. Bats are *not* birds. Now if science had said that having wings and flying makes them a form of bird, then that makes sense. In fact, it makes perfect sense.

How about Cain and his wife? Where did she come from? They say he married a sister. I won't even come to the door on that. It's moronic. However, if science said that we trace our human ancestry back to one individual, then that truth is welcome, because it makes sense.

I can look directly at this vast, intricate creation and say that it's not proof that there is a Creator. I need give no explanation. Such talk flies in the face of reason and common logic, but I don't care.

There is a reason I don't like truth. It's because it carries light, and I don't like light...unless I can control it. There is a room inside my house that I like to keep dark. Very dark. It is what I call an "adult" fantasy room. You know what I mean. That room keeps the residents here, and it keeps me in control.

I like to call evil good, and good evil. I do this because I hate absolutes, because absolutes speak of truth.

Each time I am unreasonable, I fortify my house. I love living in the House of Atheist with my other demon friends. That's because we are very welcome here. When the resident is seized by my master and taken to his permanent place, I will just move on and find another house. There are plenty out there.

Actually, I know that everything the Bible says is true. The Word of God makes me tremble. In the face of what I have said, that makes no sense. I know that...I'm just being Unreasonable.

NOTES

PREFACE

1. Copies of this booklet are available online at www.livingwaters.com.

2. Learn more about the School of Biblical Evangelism program online at www.biblicalevangelism.com/.

3. The DVD containing the video obtained with this camera is available through the Living Waters Ministry at www.livingwaters.com.

4. "Only 10 percent of the world's population claims atheism. It looks like you've managed to attract most of that population to a single blog! Truly amazing." "It's a great place to meet other atheists." http://raycomfortfood.blogspot.com/.

CHAPTER ONE

1. Stephen Hawking, *A Brief History of Time: From the Big Bang to Black Holes* (New York: Bantam Books, 1988), 127.

2. Adapted from Ray Comfort, *The Atheist Bible* (Nashville, Tennessee: Holman Bible Publishers, 2009).

3. Stephen Hawking, "The Beginning of Time," (public lecture) available at www.hawking.org.uk/pdf/bot.pdf.

4. Hawking, *Brief History of Time*, 127.

5. Quoted in John Boslough, *Stephen Hawking's Universe* (New York: Harper Collins' Avon imprint, 1989), 109.

6. Associated Press, "Telescope detects space dust," October 10, 2007, http://premium.asia.cnn.com/2007/TECH/space/10/10/cosmic.dust.ap/index.html.

7. Ibid.

8. Adapted from Ray Comfort, *How to Know God Exists* (Alachua, Florida: Bridge-Logos, 2008).

9. Charles Darwin, "The Races of Man,"in *The Descent of Man*, (1874).

10. Dan Barker, former false convert, author, critic. Cited on his biographical page on the *Rational Atheist* Web site, available at http://www.rationalatheist.com/biographies/Dan_Barker.html, accessed December 3, 2008.

11. Kirk Cameron held up a mock photo of a species-to-species transitional form during a debate with atheists on ABC's *Nightline* in April 2007.

12. *Understanding Evolution,* "What has the head of a crocodile and the gills of a fish?" May 2006, available at http://evolution.berkeley.edu/evolibrary/news060501_tiktaalik.

13. Claire Pye, *The Wild World of the Future* (Tonawanda, New York: Firefly Books, 2003).

14. Quoted in "The Whole Story," The Future is Wild Project, available at http://www.thefutureiswild.com/pdf/E01-The-whole-story.pdf.

CHAPTER THREE

1. Adapted from Comfort, *How to Know God Exists.*

CHAPTER FOUR

1. Charles Spurgeon, "The Sinner's End" (sermon delivered at the Metropolitan Tabernacle, Newington, London, England, December 28, 1862) available at http://www.biblebb.com/files/spurgeon/0486.htm.

2. Charles Spurgeon, "Sovereign Grace and Man's Responsibility" (sermon delivered at the Music Hall, Royal Surrey Gardens, Kennington, London, England, August 1, 1858) available at http://www.spurgeon.org/sermons/0207.htm.

3. Charles Spurgeon, "The Sinner's End."

CHAPTER FIVE

1.Quoted in J.H. Tiner, *Isaac Newton—Inventor, Scientist, and Teacher* (Milford, Michigan: Mott Media, 1975).

CHAPTER SIX

1. Avilable at www.livingwaters.com/Merchant2/merchant.mv?Screen=PROD&Product_Code=512.

2.*The Evidence Bible*, Ray Comfort (Bridge Logos Publishers).

3.Mohandas K. Gandhi, *An Autobiography: The Story of My Experiments with Truth*, trans. Mahadev Desai (Boston, MA: Beacon Press, 1993), Introduction.

CHAPTER SEVEN

1. *A Splitting of the Mind*, "Schizophrenia: A Dissection," available at

http://pellmel.wordpress.com/definitions-meanings/schizophrenia-adissection/.

CONCLUSION

1. See Psalm 111:10.

2. *Understanding Hinduism*, "Reincarnation," From the teachings of Sri Ramana Maharshi, edited by David Godman. Question and answer as follows: "Is it possible for a man to be reborn as a lower animal?" "Yes. It is possible, as illustrated by Jada Bharata—the scriptural anecdote of a royal sage having been reborn as a deer," available at www.hinduism.co.za/reincarn.htm.

3. "When you transcend your thinking mind in the realization of your own pure, timeless, ever-present awareness, then the illusion of time completely collapses, and you become utterly free of the samsaric cycle of time, change, impermanence, and suffering." www.buddhistinformation.com.

4. "Then those whose balance (of good deeds) is heavy, they will be successful. But those whose balance is light, will be those who have lost their souls; in hell will they abide" (Koran 23:102,103).

5. "The sacrifice of the wicked is an abomination to the Lord, but the prayer of the upright is His delight" (Proverbs 15:8).

6. See Romans 13:14.

7. Galatians 3:13.

8. Romans 8:2.

9. John 3:16.